Finding Bigfoot Indoors

Rob Knopka

Contents

FORWARD

I never intended to write this book. I started by looking for answers to the Bigfoot phenomenon and why I was seeing these things every week on my television. I wanted to know more. I thought that I could just Google something and find the answer. When I couldn't find the answer, I was puzzled. So I started to research to see if there were pieces I could string together to make a complete picture. What I found shocked me.

I first started my research looking for an easy way to locate a big creature. And I found one. Digital maps of the earth are available to everyone. These digital maps have been around for a few years and can been used for many purposes. You can look at the same area in the winter, spring, summer or fall. And you can spot deer and people and any great big animals, too.

Regarding the Bigfoot phenomena there are two factions: Believers and skeptics. I guess I was always a believer. I believe there may be undiscovered things on this planet that are still just waiting to be found. I wanted to find a group that shared similar beliefs and could provide answers to my questions.

But just like choosing a religion, there are many kinds of believers who pick and choose what they want to believe, and disregard what they don't. I thought that the probability of an unknown primate species undiscovered was pretty good. I just couldn't find a group of believers I could interact with that saw things as I did.

What I found was that I didn't match a lot of groups. They were set in their own thoughts on what Bigfoot is and how it behaves. This was not what I was experiencing or seeing, but I tried to find a close match anyway. As an outsider, I saw that the Bigfoot world has many facets. They all follow in the same general direction, but get to where they are differently. They report various types of creatures with dissimilar features, yet all are reported collectively and proclaimed as Bigfoot sightings. Each have witnesses that tell a story, with physical evidence and occasional pictures or video. And all are summarily dismissed by our esteemed scientific community leaders. This makes no sense. If I showed you bruises and a blurry video of a guy robbing a convenience store, there is a concern and interest in finding him. If I show you bruises and a blurry video of an unknown creature attack, there is ridicule. So many cases have been swept under the rug. Why?

Just for fun, I sent an email to a television show actor to help him and his group find Bigfoot after I located several on a map in his favorite Bigfoot location. He had said he had been visiting the area looking for Bigfoot and physical evidence for several years now. I thought he and his team could use a fresh lead to lift their spirits after looking unsuccessfully for so long.

I never got a response from him. I thought it was useful information. I really didn't expect I would get a reply, but I hoped he would use the map to find one. Maybe a map seemed redundant, since he has more than enough resources and high tech equipment at his disposal. Oh, well! At least I tried. Better luck next season. Stay safe. Happy hunting, guys!

One of his team members is a self-proclaimed skeptic. Or at least they are scripted and presented to the public as one. One of my objectives besides passing on good information is to give the skeptical people some facts that they can't reasonably dispute. Now I don't expect to change anyone's mind about their beliefs. I only wish to add my experience as supporting evidence to the cause. There will come a time soon when a dead Bigfoot body is presented without intervention, and will rally support to a call for species identification. But skeptics don't really need to see a dead body to convince them. They know that, but that's not their point. I thought about making their wish come true, but then decided against hunting and killing one.

Providing a Bigfoot body would create instant controversy, understandably, but it would also muddle the educational issues. Instead I prefer to challenge the skeptics to view first for themselves. They can then proceed as they have always done, which is to whine and complain without providing any valid argument. But the pictures speak for themselves. Tell me you don't see animals in your woods. Fine. At least I know that you looked.

If you read this book but don't try to look for a creature, you have a poor rebuttal. To present an argument they would have to be an active participant viewing the map using tangible evidence. OMG. And they would have to figure out for themselves what they are looking at. They would no longer be able to just sit back pompously and cry "hoax", like they do to the many Bigfoot sighting videos. And would lose their excuse to callously call "fake" like they reply to the posted Bigfoot cellphone pictures. The only thing they can do now is to make excuses for not looking at the data on their computer screen.

They may say they can't find anything that looks like a primate. Which is bull. Or they do nothing at all. Of course someone will badmouth this book without reading it because they're in denial or just plain lazy. If you have evidence, show it and let's debate its worth. If you have nothing, then just shut up. Cause reality apparently is not what you want to believe. You just want to whine.

This book is not a definitive resource for everything Bigfoot. It is not meant to be. I am new to Bigfoot research and have a lot more to learn. I'm learning more each day with each discovery. But this book has a lot of useful information that I thought would help those who hold a piece of the puzzle, and are wondering how the pieces fit together. I hope that the dedicated Bigfoot followers may benefit with this information I found as well. They spend a lot of time trying to find the answers. I just hope they will use this information responsibly.

I'm not putting these facts together to encourage crazy behavior. I'm not encouraging inexperienced people to engage wild animals in their outdoor environment. I am providing a useful method to locate and eventually identify strange animals which can be viewed in various outdoor locations. This method can help you see beyond the gates and fences. But it does not give you a right to trespass onto other people's property. It merely gives you a true snapshot of recent Bigfoot activity and where they frequent.

The best news is anonymity is not necessary when reporting your sighting. It is what it is. There is no cloak of mystery needed about the action you see. There is no ambiguity about the exact location of the creatures. There is no need to be ashamed to say what you saw. Because we can all see it too.

The GPS coordinates can be used to see someone else's animal or interesting interaction. And you can see how many there are in a given area without trekking through the woods and swamps. It is a safe method as long as you use it as intended. It is a map made available for use and it is free. So go ahead, use it and build your case.

INTRODUCTION

I have not been an avid enthusiast of the Bigfoot phenomenon until recently. Sure, I watched some programs on television and thought that maybe something out there was not yet identified. That has all changed. Now I search, I watch, I listen for all clues to purported Bigfoot behavior. I am awash of strange unexplained occurrences in the woods reported by the various media outlets and others.

To note, there has not an increase in activity. But there is an explosion of unusual events being recorded and shared outside of the conventional news media outlets we rely on to report the news. Today people are continuously uploading and providing a wide array of pictures and video online of events as they happen. More people get to see these events immediately since everyone now has upload capability and cameras on their phones. There is a phenomenal database growing stronger of Bigfoot sightings and occurrences across the internet. This is my contribution to this growing database of sightings. It is in digital format that is viewable worldwide.

Every anthropologist or zoologist wants to go to the Amazon to discover a new species. However, not one scientist is bothering to look out their kitchen window. How many sightings of strange creatures are needed before someone decides it might be important enough to investigate? How many seed research dollars can send a team to investigate right here in our own back yard? When is that going to happen?

There are a lot of amateur sleuths out there who spend a lot of their own time and money investigating certain areas. They are trying to get some definitive proof together that will tip the scales. They have the spirit and the determination to get the deed done. Unfortunately, they head out into the unknown poorly equipped and ill-informed about what to expect on their journey. I'm concerned for those adventurers, as they may be walking into situations that could have grave consequences.

Most smart people plan ahead before they go on a trip. Getting some brochures, read some literature, check online comments, and take website recommendations to name a few. Some do research to find out what they can expect to find in the vicinity around their planned destination. A few even want to know every individual aspect along their travel route and at their final destination so there are no surprises. And some just wing it…and have unrealistic expectations about what they expected when they finally get there.

This book doesn't address unrealistic expectations. It is geared more to the reasonable person who wants to know what to expect, as well as hopefully provides insight to understanding the perils in the woods. A reasonable person would want to know about unusual events and possible dangers before they go off into the wilderness. Whether or not you purposely plan an encounter in your travels, it's always wise to prepare for the unexpected. This information hopefully will help you to prepare.

ABOUT ME

I've spent a lot of time in the woods and swamps when I was a kid, and I thought I knew every animal that was out there. Now I'm not so sure what you might find out there. As people head out with their cameras and gear to search for monsters or prove their suspicions, there is always a slight chance that they might not come back. Thousands of people go missing in the National Forests every year, and no government agency or organization keeps any investigation open or active beyond the initial search phase.

No agency continues to pursue or investigates similarities or patterns regarding an area where multiple persons go missing. Sure, there is an individual missing persons report, and a search team goes out to look. But if they can't find you, you are missing. Case closed. Don't ask the Forest Service for their knowledge about where the most people go missing, or inquire about information about where you are more likely to experience Bigfoot sightings in the forest. You will get a standard agency approved response, not their personal beliefs of the event or clues to follow based on their personal experience. You are on your own.

When a sighting is reported to local law enforcement they investigate the initial complaint, and then if the news outlet hears about it the local news agencies report on it, and then the story just fizzles and goes away. No further action is warranted. There is no follow up. End of story. There appears to be no official effort on the part of any government or organization to help identify or try to explain what is really going on. This book tries to help identify and tie together some of the loose ends in this story.

If you are an experienced outdoorsman, you might already know what to expect when you spot a wild animal in the woods. However, if you cannot wrap your mind around what you are seeing, your reaction time may be delayed. You must process the unknown animal sighting data into your known animal database. This will baffle even the most experienced hunter, who has been trained to identify their target. How do you do that if you can't identify or classify what you are seeing from what you thought you already knew?

If you are a novice with an urge to catch a glimpse of elusive creatures in their natural habitat, I would strongly suggest that you use the buddy system. It is always good to have a wingman to convince you that you are not thinking clearly. A buddy can help to keep you safe. A buddy also provides you with another opinion. They will support or counter your decisions as being either a smart idea or a just plain dumb one.

As for me, I don't spend my leisure time roaming the woods or swamps much anymore. I spend it on my motorcycle in the summer, and inside at home during the winter. I roam the television channels and the internet searching for answers to this puzzle that shouldn't exist.

Over the last few years I've caught and been hooked on exploration and discovery type of shows. These shows are popular probably because everybody loves treasure hunts. They go off searching a new location each week to find something that was either lost in time or else long forgotten as the world moved on.

While some exploration shows are based upon established data or past written record, other shows rely simply upon belief. Of course I, like others I know, play the skeptic when I am told to have faith in something I cannot see. I prefer hard evidence over some "what if" scenarios, but I still will commit an hour of my time to watch people undertake an impossible task to try to prove that something is real.

I play armchair quarterback sometimes. I tell whoever is in the room at the time about how I would have done it differently. Of course my way is either a better way or an easier way, or both. Most people who play armchair quarterback with the TV set feel the same way.

I was drawn in recently by some cable television shows that were obviously playing on people's fear of the unknown. The show finds some witnesses who tell their story, and includes an animated recreation of the event. Then it ties in to the unusual or mysterious events that occurred during the investigation to the original sighting. I started following one show that seeks to find mountain creatures in every county in the state of West Virginia. It proclaims that each county has a unique woods creature of their own. Now wait. How can that be possible? So of course I was hooked each week, as I just had to watch to see what these unusual creatures all over were.

There are legends and myths throughout our history of strange creatures and unusual sightings reported throughout the world. West Virginia apparently keeps their scary creatures distinctly separated by the county lines. I don't know which baffled me more: The fact that there are so many legendary creatures living in one state, or the fact that each and every county has problems attributed to a uniquely identified different creature. When I later discovered how many creatures there actually are in West Virginia, I was astounded.

I am originally from New Jersey, the Garden State, and grew up in the southern part of the state near the Wharton State forest, which has 115,000 acres of pine trees. I had my own personal experience in those woods with the infamous Jersey Devil, a local legend of the state, while on a hunting trip as a teen. The sound of the wings flapping and the bone chilling screeching was unnerving and scary, even though I had a gun. I never did continue hunting as an adult. Not because of the Jersey Devil, mind you. Instead I justified my not wanting to hunt as not wanting to be standing in the cold mud of the swamps or freezing high in a tree stand for hours on end. If I did get a chance to shoot at something and kill it, I surely didn't want to drag it home or have to clean it. And I didn't want to be out in the woods killing things for fun. It just wasn't for me.

After I graduated high school I entered the US Army. I had three years of German in high school, so I thought I would probably end up in Germany. Nope. My first duty station was in Bayonne, New Jersey. This is the port where the serviceman's cars get loaded onto ships to go to Germany. Join the Army and see New Jersey.

After 16 months I got an overseas assignment: Panama. I ended up spending three years there. It was tropical and muggy. I canoed in the ocean around the Panama Canal locks and explored the jungle regions on the Atlantic side of the Canal Zone. For training, my squad would play aggressors and try to infiltrate an infantry camp to capture their leader. Needless to say, I spent many nights in the dark jungle moving around soldiers unnoticed and getting to my objective.

I used some copies of maps of the jungle terrain where I knew a dirt road was safely passable, and went out on many weekends exploring the jungle. It was hot hacking through brush with a machete, and it was dirty sliding down muddy hillsides, and it was scary wading waist deep through muddy streams, but it was fun overall.

On the Atlantic Ocean side of the Isthmus of Panama I would park my car at a park point I selected along a dirt road nearest to a point of interest I saw on a military map. Sometimes it would be dotted lines showing an unusual terrain feature. Sometimes it would just be a bluff overlooking a secluded cove. I would head into the jungle with my final destination being the Atlantic Ocean.

If I got lost or turned around, I could follow any moving water, since all streams there flow into the ocean. The jungle canopy makes the jungle dark and the ground cover is thick with brush and bugs. Big bugs. It's not flat ground, so it was a slow go across the hilly terrain. The ground is damp and the red mud is clay-like, so you walk some, crawl some, slide some as you go along.

In my travels I found some old unmapped Spanish ruins of a fortress that was taken out by invaders. There were rusted iron fragments and broken bottles from the 1700's, but nothing seemed worthy of keeping or taking back home. Once on a bluff overlooking the Atlantic Ocean about 25 miles west of the Gatun Locks, I found a railroad bumper overgrown in the underbrush.

After hacking away at the brush I saw that there were tracks like train tracks with rails and ties. The tracks went back into the jungle and had palm trees growing up between the tracks in the track bed. Most back roads in Panama get easily overgrown with vines and foliage bits if not continually maintained, so I knew that the tracks had been abandoned for quite some time. I was surprised that they were not on the military map, since the Panama railway did not extend this far away. I followed the tracks away from the bluff through a ravine and around a quarter turn and found a collapsed bunker dug into the side of a hill. I peered inside.

There was nothing of any value remaining in the bunker that I could see. Later I learned that the long forgotten rail tracks and bunker was part of the canal defense during World War 2. There were big guns on the tracks that would be rolled out of the bunkers to the bluff for protection from invaders. I always found something interesting when I ventured into the jungle.

I never took a camera, which I regret now. At the time I was young and dumb. I wore sneaks, a pair of cutoffs, a t-shirt and carried only a machete. . I traveled light. That was sufficient to go exploring. No GPS, camera gear or backpack. As I proceeded through the thick terrain, then I heard the ocean…I knew I was close to the end of the jungle portion.

When I stepped out onto the beach I would find a spot and rest to take in the ocean view for a while. There are miles and miles of sandy beach without another soul around. Some points and alcoves had coral outcroppings jutting into the ocean. If there was coral on the beachhead I would poke around looking for sea creatures. Baby sharks used to get caught in tidal pools of the corral, stranding them for a while in the warm salty pockets until the tide returned them later to the ocean.

Below the Spanish ruins I found earlier, there were cannon balls embedded in the coral from some long forgotten battle against invading ships. It was very cool to explore. Then I would mosey back to the road that met the beach, and hike the road back to my car at the park point. I never did an overnight trip, only day excursions. The jungle was pitch-black at night, and orientation was difficult without a compass. I never slept out in a tent overnight as a civilian because of the huge bugs. I spent several weeks at a stretch living in the jungle when we had war games. Something about having to spend time in tents at work makes you not want to sleep in tents on your days off.

The howler monkeys in the jungle were the best to mess with. As they watched me curiously and followed me through the jungle, I would sometimes backtrack around them and surprise them. They were comical to watch. They always retreated hastily as you approached them. They would watch you from a distance, and never dare approach while you were in the area. Occasionally they would bellow, but I never did know why. It was a deep and throaty howl that sounded scary if you didn't see them first.

They were also the thieves of the neighborhood. They would take loose things from your yard when you weren't around. Some of the new neighbors weren't told fast enough. If you were outside at the time, everything was normal. But if you left to go to the store or something, there were things missing when you got back. You always had to clean up after a party if you wanted to keep your stuff. Just for the record the monkeys liked to take Christmas decorations and garden gnomes.

That's about all I've known about monkey behavior before this. I'm no Jane Goodall, but I know an obvious pattern when I see it. And the first creatures I saw looked a lot like monkeys. I couldn't find any similar species from the known primates. I'm guessing that some of the creatures I see in the woods are either a distant relative of primates or something similar due to the behavior they seem to exhibit.

Once species identification begins and definitive species type verification is concluded, maybe we can clear up and classify all the unidentified matches of DNA clogging the system. Most DNA hair samples that have been gathered and processed so far have been identified as a "no match to the known database" because they haven't been recognized as a species yet. But…anthropologists and zoologists haven't even looked.

I saw a wide variety of vibrantly colored pretty birds in the jungle, which I expected. What I expected but didn't see were very many snakes. I would say that I saw more snakes in my yard and my neighbor's yards on the military base than I ever saw in the jungle. Maybe because they were easier to see with the lawns trimmed. When I went through the jungle I was purposely noisy as I hacked through the jungle brush. I guess that the noise helped keep them away. I didn't want to be surprised by a snake hanging down in my face along with the vines.

They had a snake in Panama they called the "two step", because that is about as far as you could walk if you were bitten by one. I don't recall the scientific name. But I wasn't worried. That kind of snake was reported to be living further in the interior of the peninsula instead of where I explored and lived along the coastal region. Snakes keep you alert anyway, checking where you walk anytime you go out into the wild where they live.

My favorite animal was the three - toed sloths, which I picked up and handled on many occasions. I would help them along on their way if they were in a busy area. Many times I stopped my car and helped them cross a paved road. They are so darned slow! Unless they fear you, you are fine to extend a stick for them to grab. They are not that heavy. They have some huge claws that could cut you open if you spook them. And they do smell funky. I saw many cool things during my jungle excursions and enjoyed being an adventurer. Now here I go later in life messing with monkeys (or a distant relative of them) and again exploring the unknown.

I will have to say that the various Bigfoot-Sasquatch-Yeti shows I have been watching lately have strongly pushed my cognitive process limit to find commonality between these types of creatures. They all have similar traits and profiles. They are huge fur-covered bipedal animals that live in the areas that human rarely visit. The distant mountains, the backwoods swamps and the deep forests are their world.

I made the decision to go out and stomp in some woods nearby that appeared to have activity. I just had to satisfy my curiosity that they do exist. I wanted to separate the facts from the fiction for myself. But my excursion was well worth it. What I saw changed my life forever. I now had my own Bigfoot sighting, and a story to tell.

However posting the information online for comments and intelligent discussion was a complete disaster. I had come back from my field excursion with some so-so pictures and video with maybe two or three seconds of actual good stuff. I expected to share my experience to get their opinions on what kind of animal it could be, if it wasn't a monkey. It could hold swamp grass shoots in its hand while balancing and crawling on a log. I posted it to a Bigfoot group blog that professed to research and investigate sightings and experiences. But it didn't go well.

THE LOST POST

The first to respond to my post was the antagonist, who was waiting to pounce. I still don't understand why he trolled this group in particular. To make a long story short, he drew all over my pictures with a red pen and said it looked like a dragon. Are you kidding me? This is the support group that holds the answers to my questions?

After three defensive responses from me and three more ludicrous replies from him, I stopped. I thought wait...I didn't need to defend what I saw. I was only sharing information, and hoping for some positive feedback. But the cavalry of intelligence never arrived. I checked back for over an hour, and all I got was a response from a fool. This type of support was not expected. I felt hurt that someone would demean my evidence on a site that was dedicated to research and investigation. I didn't wait any further for some morsel of encouragement to arrive, or some fast comment about similar sightings to appear. In frustration I took down both my picture posts and the video link from the group's site and just quit the group.

I searched for a more intelligent group. I scrutinized the comments made by the members. The Bigfoot blogs I visited seemed rampant with antagonists and critics. I tried another one. They pounced on my sighting like a cat on a mouse. The first response was quick and put the post into a negative light. My first thought was that these people probably join this type of specialty group just to harass and demean others. Maybe they need to stroke their ego by putting others down, or find the anonymity of the internet an easy way to behave poorly. I deleted my post, frustrated and confused. They seemed to intentionally deter people from sharing their experience with others. A decent open conversation with group members about an experience wasn't possible. The lesson I learned was not to try to seek advice or encouragement from these groups. Now I see why people don't report a Bigfoot sighting.

Conversely, the nature of the commentary and the persistence of the harasser lead me to believe that there is more to this story than meets the eye. Who is this guy? Is this a screening room to minimize impact and deter reporting? Is it the site, or the members? As I scrolled through the comments, the same people keep showing up. Why would they keep a member that ridicules everyone's posts? That made no sense. I dug a little deeper, and found out that my antagonist was also a moderator. OK. It is a front for something else. But what?

Follow the money. There are those in the world that will not be happy when they find out that their real estate investment property is an active nesting site for an unidentified indigenous animal. There's a lot of money invested in real estate. Do disclosure laws exempt Bigfoot? The animals have always been there. So, what's the big deal? Why can't people openly discuss their sightings and experience without these clown comments? On many sites the comment section seems to each have at least one clown posting multiple comments badgering all responders with rude replies. The initial item of interest trails off. The well-intentioned report of an earnest successful explorer is hopelessly lost in a big mess. Bullied into oblivion.

It has been a rough road exploring the Bigfoot phenomena. It is not easy to locate facts based upon reasoning or, as I just mentioned, locating an intelligent ongoing discussion among any of the groups of self-proclaimed Bigfoot fans. Nothing is effectively analyzed, therefore nothing is concluded. Fact checking seems to be nonexistent in this field. There are a lot of self-anointed experts, mind you, but they don't provide many verifiable facts. Here is an example. He saw one in the woods once, and never found bones, so they must bury their dead. What kind of logic is that?

Whether they are in a group or in a blog, I know that every member (except the trolls) that joined holds at least one valuable piece to the puzzle. Each newcomer that visits brings some key element of information to add. But the system of education is flawed. It is hopelessly infested with trolls who mock and denigrate what the group tries to accomplish.

Every posting I saw that started with a new piece of evidence presented was systematically kneed in the nuts by some clown who brought nothing to the table. Using no factual basis for their argument, these antagonists bring a sincere search for answers to a grinding halt with their condescending comments. I was sad that I could gain little information on sites that were started with such well-meaning intentions. Unfortunately the puzzle piece that last posted remains unanswered as to how it fits into the overall picture. It is with these scant pieces of information and commonly referenced works that I tried to put together to make the puzzle whole.

If you aren't aware by now, it is also difficult to have a reasonable conversation about new Bigfoot evidence in the company of a mixed group. Closed minded people are adamant that their way of thinking is correct. Most of these people are of the opinion that because they haven't seen one in person with their own eyes, they must not exist. These are the fools who pay good money to see plastic monkey parts in a freezer. I hate to tell them that they probably won't get to see one ever, because Bigfoot can smell a big butthole a mile away. And I think to myself while they rant that I'm talking to one. But I bite my lip and don't say what I'm thinking to them. But I should. It's not easy to make everyone happy about this whole Bigfoot thing. It is a lot to digest.

There's going to be a lot of people unhappy when they realize how many animals are really out there. And some people will be concerned where the animals are living and where they go when they mill about. I know where they are, and I'm not worried. But there is going to be a lot of drama by the unknowing population who don't believe these creatures exist. These people cannot even fathom how a Bigfoot can continue to exist (with their basic survival methods and rudimentary skills) in this day and age. But seeing is definitely believing.

Keep in mind that fact that Bigfoot has lived here longer than you. Bigfoot creatures have been sighted and recorded since pre-Columbian times. Bigfoot has adorned ancient pottery and totem poles. Long before your house was built they were probably living in that space. Humans have bumped them from their territory into their existing spaces, where they feel comfortable living without your intrusion. As a note, I am not a proponent of stalking them or causing unnecessary intrusion. This type of activity may backfire on the unprepared adventurer.

When I had my sighting, I didn't go down to the swamp after I thought it had left. When I got home, I saw on the video that two adults were also watching the small one I was watching. I was glad I didn't try to catch up with it. I used caution. You should too. These creatures have survived the great Native American hunters with bows and arrows. They continue to survive today having hunters with guns busting through their sanctuary and disturbing their habitat. They live in rudimentary conditions that you couldn't. They are the epic true survivors. And when you encounter them, surprise them, or confront them, you are the foremost immediate threat to their survival. Remember that.

There are currently plenty of Bigfoot and Sasquatch websites and numerous blogs on the internet today with hundreds of sightings and images posted. I am sure that you have seen some. I have visited many of these sights hoping to find answers to my questions. I even joined a couple of groups that claimed a collective interest in finding answers to the Bigfoot mystery. But they were also disappointing.

They all have their weak points. They all contain a piece of the puzzle. But each one proclaims mastery of the mystery. The sites claim ownership of the entire species and dictate what rules to follow based upon their beliefs. They provide incorrect data as fact. They attribute animals with human traits acting with a human logic, which is unreasonably sound and scientifically implausible.

Some resemble a club of fellowship that just wants to meet others with a similar story to tell, which is good. A few are even realistic enough to warn of the dangers that a wild animal can exhibit in their natural habitat, which is very sound advice. But a small amount of these groups incredibly still believe that there is only ONE Bigfoot out there. That type of club must obviously be for the novice, or for kids. They treat Bigfoot as their pet. That isn't good. Have you seen my pet?

Even the largest most popular websites claim ownership of Bigfoot itself as their prized possession and give paternal advice on how you should treat their Bigfoot. They should not be encouraging inexperienced people to go into the woods. There are people who aren't observant. I've seen their videos. I'm still not certain which Bigfoot these sites claim is theirs. I've seen a lot of them, and not one had a collar. If they want to claim one as their mascot, I can respect that. If I can give one, then you can have one. All of the Bigfoot I saw like peanut butter and apples. I'm guessing yours doesn't? Therefore, using this skewed logic I guess all the rest I saw besides yours are mine.

On these various websites I visited, the intent of the search is basically the same, but the processing and digestion of the information obtained is very different. Every site still desires a dead physical body as positive proof of existence, but not one site goes as far as to suggest or encourage someone try to capture one or kill one. The final comment on each piece of the puzzle is the same as the small group's comments. Anything less than a complete dead body is either a photo which can be faked or a video which can be staged. Subtle, but bullying nonetheless. Evidence dismissed.

You weren't there. You didn't see what they saw. Why didn't you take more pictures or just shoot it, they say. Easier said than done. Where is your experience posted? How many times have you seen something and wished you brought your camera? Or had enough battery life left. It's always easy to call bullshit from the comfort of your living room couch. Feed the trolls, and they still want more. No scientific evidence is ever presented or discussed, and never with an open mind to learn.

Let the trolls try to pick apart all the pictures and all the activity, as they view each creature using Apple, Bing or Google. If they are so smart, why haven't they done some research on the subject? So what if Bigfoot was there 3 months ago or there last fall. It was still there. Go ahead, wise guy, disprove it. The lame story about a man in a monkey suit repeated too many times won't hold up here. Long ago I gave up counting all the deer I saw in the woods, and not too long ago I gave up counting all the Bigfoot in the woods, too. I still haven't seen any dragons, though.

OTHERWORLDLY CREATURES

It's not considered to be science unless you research the facts and analyze the evidence before drawing your conclusion. While researching the Bigfoot data and posted material, I have come across some "otherworldly" beliefs about why Bigfoot is elusive. While I find some of the rationalization for nonexistence is a bit farfetched, I think some of the supernatural or the multi-dimensional explanations for Bigfoot sightings are really out there in another dimension. Until solid physical evidence or supporting video or photos are offered, it can only be seen as a theory.

I could find no factual basis to begin to analyze this type of information concerning inter-dimensional Bigfoot creatures in a logical way. I know that there are other creatures besides Bigfoot roaming the earth that are still a mystery. I just can't get a Bigfoot connection tied to the supernatural realm. If Bigfoot is visible to everyone, as I am presenting in this book, then they cannot be somewhere else like in another dimension or a spirit world while their picture is presently being taken. Unless they exist in two worlds simultaneously. I guess that may be possible. I haven't seen any show or site present evidence or provide a starting point for an otherworldly Bigfoot existence. I did hear callers on Coast to Coast radio on a podcast who talk about inter-dimensional beliefs, but I didn't see a connection. Most of the other callers presented their view that Bigfoot is just an old school flesh and blood, shy and elusive creature.

I used the cable television shows about locating Bigfoot type creatures as a starting point. I've been entertained by them for years. I don't think it's scientific, but some people get paid to watch television on grants. I wonder if I can get back pay for my vast experience. Probably not. Oh, well. It just got me thinking. I disagreed with their method of searching each week. And I figured out why. Now don't get me wrong. I admire them in their diligence tromping around in the woods at night. They persist in search of some great video footage for sweeps week. And I would not disregard their opinion based upon their physical evidence along the way. I probably used some of their efforts as a basis for my own beliefs. But I would suggest to them that they try to use some stealth instead of cacophonous behavior to acquire up-close video footage.

I am suggesting stealth only because I used it successfully in my first field sighting of the elusive ones. Some people claim to have spent years searching with little result. I would have given up if I searched continuously without hope of success. I would have given up after a few outings without any exciting results. While the evidence I obtained during my sighting wasn't as good as I had hoped, I was content nonetheless that I acknowledged Bigfoot creatures were present right where I thought they would be. Who could ask for anything more?

I do hope to get better video footage during my next field excursion. Yes, I am hooked, and have a plan. I don't plan to camp in their area, but I need to get some better video footage for myself. I'm not going to chase them, or startle them. I'm not going to stalk them or confront them, either. Something passive, just to get some footage. I plan to wait until after hunting season, of course. I was thinking maybe a couple of hours after a light snowfall would be a good time to track them, if I want to research in that direction. Maybe practice first with the video camera will make my second attempt better. Bumbling in the woods trying to figure out how to operate someone else's camera for the first time is not the ideal way to obtain great footage.

I probably would have done better taking pictures with my cell phone, which I am more familiar with. There are a lot of things I would have done differently. But in the moment, you do what you think is right. You are nervous, and your adrenalin is pumping. If no one likes the pictures, oh well! I know now what to expect. I know now what I have to do to get steadier pictures. And I know better how to proactively react next time.

I feel kind of sad that the characters on documentary shows are misled by poor or inaccurate research. I am getting mine right from the source. Here is proof that money can't buy everything. I found out where the creatures live, where they walk, and where they play. I know I can't fault anyone for using bad information to make decisions who just doesn't know any better. Somebody wrote it down, and somebody else read it. It is what it is. For entertainment purposes only.

If you have good location information you save a lot of time. This method of locating animals in the woods is not subjective. It is actual viewing of an event that occurred. For the experienced explorer, using this data is a time-saving technique, a gold mine for searching through the woods or swamps looking for tracks. The path to the water source would have the freshest track information for casting some footprints.

It is also good evidence that the creature you see once stood exactly on those GPS coordinates on the date that the map was created. There won't be the lame old argument about people in gorilla suits here. How many gorilla suits were rented in April 2014 during the camera flyover? There will still be the people too lazy to open up the program but still talk their crap about it. Let them refute the evidence. Just like those people who believe that there are no large hairy creatures roaming the woods. They can debate until the cows come home, but they provide no facts or substance.

Yep, the naysayers are always going to believe what they want to believe…even when they find Bigfoot with their own computer. This book isn't much help for them, since they aren't looking for answers, only arguments. But it should help you. You can see everything for yourself and then decide what you want to do. Hopefully it won't be anything crazy.

I'm glad that I found this reliable method of finding and identifying the location of these animals. With limited time and funds, it helped to improve the chance of a successful sighting. It would be even greater if there was a live version in real time. Now I can pinpoint any previously sighted creature's location independently without relying on vague roadside reports from anonymous witnesses.

I can safely observe these animals as they behave in their natural habitat. I can document their traits and appearance, and interpret their behavior without relying on second hand statements from frightened homeowners or baffled tourists. I don't think that a month living in a tent would get the same results. I can use multiple year data to verify their movement within the area or track migration patterns seasonally, or use annual time frames to count the group size. All of which can be done at home from the comfort of a cushy couch.

You too can view the facts based upon what you see right at home on your computer screen. If you are inclined to be adventuresome, you can plan your next trip with a little bit more accurate information about where you want to go. You can enter the coordinates and walk to the spot that has some possible evidence. You already saw it was standing there, and saw what it was doing when it was there. Pretty cool, huh? I thought so.

With a drink and a snack I can search relentlessly for them. Life is good.

THE CALLING GAME

While watching another season of endless searching for the elusive shy one, I chuckled to myself when the guys on the show were walking through the woods at night and stopped at a tree. They started hitting the tree with a wooden stick they had brought. But first they called someone in another area of the woods on a radio to tell them that they were going to doing it. Then they called back on the radio to see if the noise was heard by the other group.

Next the guys cranked up an amplifier to blast some prerecorded sounds. Then they radioed back to get an acknowledgement from the other group. They claimed they were trying to attract a big hairy woods creature to their location. Are they serious? Unfortunately, yes. Then they get another brainstorm. They decide to mimic a monster screaming or werewolf howling and do it loud enough to echo across the valley to nearby mountains. There. That should bring them running. The actors say that they are duplicating some "known event". In five years of the show's existence, I haven't seen this known event occur. It wasn't successful this time.

The mission: They are making these sounds that they think an animal will recognize as another animal and respond to. I am baffled that they attempt to get a wild animal to reply. Let me get this right. Instead of looking for a creature, let's just call him. OK, I know the howl will work for coyotes. You can get a coyote to howl back, if you howl first. But will he come running? Is this the prevailing logic for finding a Bigfoot in the woods? Set up your cameras and call him over for an interview? I know it is entertainment. I certainly found it funny. It just doesn't make sense.

But what if the noise you are blasting across the valley is recognized by the animals as a signal to flee the area? What if the amplifier hiss and noise is recognized as a human thing? This plan would be like someone yelling "fire" and wondering why everyone immediately left the area. They will never get any animals to come when they call. And of course…they haven't. Maybe they are smart. If I heard a jingle from an ice cream truck played over an amplifier, I would only go a block or two before I realized that something wasn't right. It's a cruel trick. And it doesn't seem to work so well. Campers get a better response from Bigfoot type creatures by having a flickering camp fire burning. Maybe they should try what has been proven to work.

As for the screaming and howling that is amplified through loudspeakers believed as a known noise made from these creatures: I don't think anyone REALLY KNOWS what the call means. We can guess and ponder, but unless we see a definite action directly related to the call, we cannot say for sure what the message of the call is. My research of finding these creatures indoors doesn't really cover this. But can we get some logic to prevail?

I am just viewing creatures from the comfort of my couch, so I have nothing to support or refute the use of a game call. Does the game call used say "Come over here", or "Don't come over here"? It isn't mating season you know. If it was, and you knew that the call defined the action of come hither as a result of the call, I would agree with that assessment. But to think that replicating a noise and expecting a result will be successful is like someone recording a bulldozer sound and expecting to see a construction crew come. Is that your best "A" game? It's trial and error, if you ask me. You don't seem to be catching those bees with your vinegar. I'm just saying.

I think all the creatures in the woods have had different life experiences, so they would act independently different to sounds you make in the woods. Some have probably never heard the sound of a barking dog. Some have never heard an airplane. Some have never experienced people. If they see you making a noise and associate it with you, they might think all people do the same. This is identification by association.

Before I had heard a loon, I didn't know what to expect. When I heard one in Maine for the first time, I said what in the hell was that? And once I knew that's what they sounded like, and heard them over and over, I got used to the sound and never winced. Ask someone who thinks a Bigfoot call would work for their reasoning to use the call. I haven't heard of any successful sighting following a recorded playback. I think they just got some bad advice. Maybe if they play it backwards? It works for deer.

I put deer whistles on the bumper of my car to scare away deer on the road. Needless to say, two weeks later I hit a deer with my car. When I went back to the automotive store, I complained that they didn't work. Instead of chasing the deer, it seemed like I must have been calling them. The guy behind the counter said with a straight face "There you go. You must have put the deer whistles on backwards". I guess if the recording doesn't work for attracting Bigfoot, try playing it backwards. It worked on the White Album.

What if the recorded scream they played over the amplified system back from mountaintop to mountaintop is actually saying: "I'm King of These Woods, Get Out or Else"? I guess that this is where the true faith part comes in. Believe in doing what you think is the right thing…In the middle of the woods…LOUDLY…At night. And good luck with that!

What do you suggest would the call be for "Dinnertime, We Have Free Food here"? Cue that one up. That call would be the one I WOULD use. It always worked for me, even today I still respond to the dinnertime call. If their recorded scream actually says "Dinnertime, We Have Unarmed Campers Here"…that recorded call would be the one that I would definitely NOT USE. Not being an expert but wanting to know more, I Googled a search on primate behavior. Guess what I found. Most experts in primates were advising that the calls bellowed by primates (possible similar behavior) toward other primates are a CHALLENGE to fight for either dominance or territory. Uh-oh. That can never be good.

I wonder if these actors on these television shows have reasonably good health insurance. I sure hope they do, because if they are challenging a primate to a battle, they had better bring more to the fight than their big wooden knocking stick. And if one shows up, they had better be prepared to defend. You know what I hear? I hear banjos.

The good news: If they find out you are a human calling and they've already experienced fear from human interaction before then you might have a chance to escape from the woods unharmed.

The bad news: There is more than one out there, and you are intimidating them in the dark, and they fight like ANIMALS.

Let's assume for argument's sake that the wood knock means something to all these animals with various life experiences and the howl and the scream means something to them as well. So who is this Bigfoot communicating with…of course, another Bigfoot. Those in the loop know that sustainability requires a male and a female to make baby ones.

If you think that there is only one Bigfoot, you are a definite novice and need to relearn some basic procreation standards. There is more than one, and there are many different types.

I continue to do research to get a definitive sampling of them, as there are significantly more than one species. There is currently a sustainable population of creatures roaming the woods, and some of these are encroaching on the human territory and are causing problems.

It has been seen for hundreds of years, but they are not hundreds of years old. It has been seen all over the world at various times of the year, but it can only run about twenty-five miles an hour cross country. It is sometimes red, sometimes white, sometime brown, sometimes black, sometimes gray and sometimes mixed.

If you think there is only one, I apologize first for your bad information. If you have spent a lifetime searching for one, I can give you the best method to locate the right place to go. If you are looking for a particular one in your neighborhood, you can find it this way.

If you already are aware and enthused that there are thousands of them from coast to coast, then continue on. If you are lost or confused at this point, don't despair. Set this book down for now and seek advice or consoling about the mysterious creatures who roam the woods from someone you can trust. This information that I am giving you will give you the ability to see for yourself what I have seen. It is not for the faint of heart or the squeamish. It's wild, and it's real.

THE WOOD KNOCK LOGIC

We can speculate that these creatures have developed rudimentary communication skills comparable to animals at the zoo since they interact daily with others in their group. Both in captivity and also in the wild, similar primates are known and have been documented to use both overt and subtle noises combined with gestures to communicate. I haven't found a comparative study yet to suggest that the ones in the wild have developed or have the same capacity to develop the same level of skills as ones in captivity. I may be mixing apples with oranges when I suggest that primate behavior is prevalent in a Bigfoot type creature. I'm only using this behavior as a known and previously documented form of demonstrated animal behavior that can be causally related to these bipedal animals.

This is my first reaction: I think the wood knock is a signal that a danger is present. Beware. Maybe it means to prepare, to pick up rocks and take up arms for protection from intruders. Who knows? I would be really wary of using this signaling technique to an animal, any animal, without knowing the consequences.

I haven't been able to figure out what makes people believe that all these creatures have the same habits. There is no logical reason to assume that all these animals from various parts of the earth recognize the same signal. Did they all go to a wood-knock class at Bigfoot University? Or did they learn it from the elders as a tradition that was passed on from creature to creature as they became old enough to learn it. If it means something important, can it be a universal practice that signifies a unification of the group or the finding of the lost?

And if there is a variation to its meaning; would a Yeti, a Sasquatch, a Swamp Ape and a Bigfoot all know what a particular wood knock means? Again, I don't have enough study information available to draw a logical conclusion to this type of action. Perhaps those who go into the field studies can provide a more definitive answer. I only know that all attempts to call a Bigfoot by wood knocking have failed. Some have heard responses and attributed the responses to their action, but they are presuming that one action has led to the other. Until we know what happens to cause a wood knocking to happen, and what happens as a consequence of those who hear it, we won't be certain to link these events together.

I think holding a stick at one end and striking another object to make a sound would have to be a learned behavior, like children learn how to use a bat by watching a baseball game. Wait, no. Bad idea. We don't want any Bigfoot batting rocks at us while we are in the woods. That would be horrible. Please do not give Bigfoots free tickets to a baseball game. They can howl and scream all they want, but the rocks just make it dangerous.

Banging on a tree is a distinctive behavior, but can it be independently learned? Did the creatures from Oregon who vacation in Washington get shown how to tap on a tree? I think it is presumptive to assume that animals from different areas all communicate the same. When people began their communication skills they didn't all have the same language or write the same in different areas. Why would you think these creatures are any different?

They should have intuitive skills, adaptive skills, and learned behavior skills. Knocking on trees seems to be a learned skill. There is no intuitive need. There is no adaptive need, unless you are knocking fruit from a tree that you can't reach. It is a learned skill if you want to signal an animal up in the tree to come down by knocking on the tree. I think this is the most practical reason to knock on a tree. Get the little ones to come down, so they don't have to climb the tree to get them. Another practical application of knocking on a tree is they may be trying to impress another creature with their might or resourcefulness. Those types of behaviors would also be learned from either elders or each other. But it can't be universal unless they commute.

Theoretically, if tapping or knocking was a universally accepted communication method, there would have to be a continuous network across the country, like smoke signals and drums were used by people long ago to communicate over distance. If a creature heard a wood knock today, I am not sure that they would know how to reproduce the sound without seeing it performed first. Therefore, unless these animals are mimicking human behavior of swinging hammers or bats, I don't see a universal connection to their wood knocking behavior.

If I was in the woods trying to communicate a warning to you without being discovered, I would try to alert you by using a natural nonintrusive sound, which the wood knock is. It makes sense if you are being smart and using your wits. A naturally occurring sound which could just be brushed away as being a tree branch falling or a random tree falling in the woods and striking another a tree. If they are clever enough to employ natural sounds as warnings or signals, we are dealing with a higher form of intelligence.

It reminds me of when I was in the Boy Scouts. In Boy Scouts we made the sound of an owl using our cupped hands as a way to signal others within range of the sound. It was a natural nonintrusive sound that could be dismissed by someone who didn't know we were communicating. I'm sure it has roots in the Native American culture as I recall. It was a signal, and everyone in our group knew what it meant when we heard it.

GRUNTS ON THE GROUND

Since my first sighting in October 2014 in the swamp, I've gotten antsy and want to see more. After work I sometimes drive to a location where I know they are active, just a short hop from where I work. I coast to a stop, get out of my truck, close the door quietly and listen for the sounds of movement in the trees.

The area I go to is along some power lines with a few hundred acres of posted property. There is a pond on one end, and a swamp on the other side of the power lines. I've heard of people who have gone in there with ATV's and explored, but I haven't gone into the woods myself. If hunters go in there, they do so illegally. It is like a sanctuary for the animals.

If you sit still and listen for a few minutes you can start to hear the sounds of the woods. The birds and the frogs and the distinct sounds of things that you would expect to hear. I hang around here about a half hour each time and scour the wooded tree line and the treetops for movement. The stickers under the power lines are nasty. The access road is full of mud holes and briars. Since I don't want to trash my truck getting in and out, I just park in a turnaround under the wires. This is my unarmed safety zone. Sometimes I'm lucky and will hear a grunt or a snort. Sometimes I get nothing. There aren't any bears near here. There aren't any wild hogs, either. The sound I hear is too deep a tone for a deer or a mocking bird. Guess what that noise is coming from.

Last March I took a drive after work because it snowed. I wanted to see if anyone made footprints across the road. I traveled to my after work hot spot, rolled down the window and drove really slow. The sunlight was low and it looked pretty in the woods. As I rolled along, I heard a bird warble. I hadn't heard it before, but it reminded me of a tropical bird. The sun was shining, a bird was warbling, and it was a pleasant cruise. No tracks out into the road, though. Oh, well. I went home. After I ate, I was reading on my laptop in bed when I started listening to a blog radio. All of a sudden, the warbling started. The noise is claimed to be present during Bigfoot activity.

I've noticed a large yellow bird present in various Bigfoot groups online, and I wondered if there was a connection. I researched the ornithology database and came up empty handed. I searched for mystery birds, and that too was a dead end. The bird sound seemed out of place outside of a tropical area. I have pics of it flying and sitting, but I didn't make the connection until now. Another piece of the puzzle.

But, back to the grunts. For some odd reason, it makes me smile when I hear the grunts come out. I don't know what the grunt noise means. Or what causes them to grunt. Maybe they smell me. The noises aren't part of my research, but I like the acknowledgement that something is making its presence known. Knowing that they are there doing their monkey business without getting jostled by hunters or being hounded by hunting dogs kind of makes me smile.

NOISES HEARD AT WORK

At work last week, I heard a scream around 3:30 in the morning, while I was outside smoking a cigarette. It was like you hear in a horror movie: A high pitched blood curdling scream that trailed off in about four seconds. It could have been human, I'm not sure. It started loud and shrill.

The woods are posted in the wooded areas around the industrial park by the county, and there are no roads in or places to park along the road for three miles, so I doubt if there were people back there. There are no turnoffs into the woods. All the paved roads have curbs and guardrails.

I had previously checked Google maps across the last four years of their digital data and found no activity close around my work place. I was both disappointed and yet somehow relieved. That doesn't preclude there is nothing roaming there now, just that I haven't seen anything obvious in the woods within a mile or more from my work. That night I walked to the end of the parking lot in the direction of the scream and listened, but I didn't hear anything else.

I was talking to one of my bosses at work about things I saw going on in the woods. When we finished talking and he left, a coworker came up to me and said he overheard our conversation about Bigfoot type creatures. He asked if I knew of any Bigfoot type creatures in West Virginia, which is where his girlfriend lives. I said that West Virginia was the first place that I had found some.

He said that the other night his girlfriend heard screams coming from the woods near her house. Did I know of any in that area? I asked him for the location. He told me, and I told him to use Google maps to show me where it is. Since I was at work, I don't have administrative rights to download or use Google Earth on their computers. That's OK, because I would spend too much time looking for monkeys instead of doing what I am supposed to be doing anyway.

So, he pulls up the location on his computer with Google maps. I say to him let me sit down. I tap down to descend down to 500 feet near his girlfriend's house. Across the street I see some. "See this", I said. Here's one…and here's one. I couldn't tell if they were male or female. She definitely had activity in her area. I panned slowly around her neighborhood and saw some more.

He said I don't see how you find them. I told him the secret. I told him you just have to look for the color variation of the tan within the green foliage and then look for the smooth lines of a figure. It isn't bumpy like the leaves. It is curvy and oval or rounded. Look for something that doesn't belong in the woods: Smooth texture.

He then showed me his family acreage in the same area, like where the relatives all live in the same valley next to a mountain. He asked if I could check the area to see if there was more. I said OK.

THREE IN A TREE

That day after work I had forgotten about it until later. I was supposed to check an area for a coworker for Bigfoot activity. When I remembered, I pulled up Google maps on my laptop and started a search. It is a rural road with houses on one side and a mountain slope on the other. I searched within a mile of the address I was given.

I saved and printed about twenty bitmap pictures of the area. Some were classic pictures of a Bigfoot mom enjoying her babies. Two pictures I saved for him were of playgrounds with young ones swinging on the crossed tree trunks. One picture showed three cubs all climbing the same tree. I thought that one was cute. One picture showed several walking down an old unused trail across the road from the house.

I offered him the color prints I made to take to his girlfriend. When he saw the prints, he thanked me. He said he told his girlfriend that the noises were made by a Bigfoot. He told her that he also saw the Bigfoot on the computer. I told him I found roughly one hundred in the mountainous area around her house. Oh, nice, he said. I said don't forget to tell her they have been there way longer than she was. It was the best advice I could offer after breaking the news.

He said he has been through those woods hundreds of times, and hasn't seen one. He hunts there. I asked him did he ever look up. He said no, not really. Most hunters aren't checking in the trees for animals. The hunters only search on one plane: ground level. Who looks for game in the trees? Maybe a squirrel or raccoon hunter does. The old growth trees in this area are over one hundred foot tall. If dogs scare them or chase them, where do you think they go? Up.

NIGHT VISION

So next I research primate vision online, looking for things like how primates see colors and specifically if they can see differently than humans. While I'm reading I note that almost all primates are not nocturnal, and they see the same way humans do. They look ahead with both eyes focused to determine depth. OK. No extra infrared vision or special perception. They are not known to have cat vision, dog vision, or deer vision.

So where did this nocturnal business come from? Why would they be moving around at night as the shows suggest? Is it an effective use of cover of darkness as a learned behavior? Or is it a method of least resistance to move unseen. Maybe they use the cover of night to raid the farm fields for food? It's a smart way to get armloads of fresh vegetables without detection. The farmer blames the deer. Farmer shoots the deer. It's all good.

On the TV they love taking their noisy actors and camera crews in tow through the woods at night. On one particular show they go hooting and hollering down a dirt road full speed in their off-road vehicles to drive the creatures to their freshly baited trap. Maybe the local primates are seen at night because they are annoyed at all the ATV's rolling through their quiet area at night? They had to check out what is going on. If I was camping, I would have checked out the commotion myself.

I am listening to Sasquatch blog radio on the internet while I am searching the maps for the best Bigfoot pictures. On the radio they talk of Bigfoot being able to see in the infrared. They use trail cameras as their example. Let me tell you my story about trail cams.

I went to a store to price a trail cam and see how many pixels I can get for a reasonable price. While trying it in the store I was surprised to hear it make a noise. I told the salesperson that I wanted one that didn't make noise. There isn't one. I can't buy a quiet camera. The salesman said the manufacturers do that so that you know it is working. I want one that was silent. Apparently one that is silent doesn't exist. This might be why animals look at the trail camera. It makes noise at them.

Another bad point about trail cams is that in order to provide motion detection, it has to sense movement. It does that by ultrasound. It is a high pitched whine. You can hear it. You can sense the mild pressure on your eardrums.

If the trail cam is set up for night viewing, it has a light. Granted, it is visible as red. We can't see the white infrared light it emits. But we can see the red. So can the animals.

So, if you are in the dark woods at night and hear a high whine and as you approach you see a blinking red light, what would you think? This is not something that belongs in the woods. This is something foreign. This is something that needs to be checked out. And if it is placed around 8 foot high and you are eight foot tall, guess what? It is eye level. You are going to check it out. So is Bigfoot.

Bigfoot cannot avoid trail cameras. But they do avoid you. They avoid you because you smell funny to them. You smell like people. They can smell you at least a quarter mile away without a breeze. If you are in the woods and touching things, your scent is present and it lingers. Hunters know this, and try to mask their scent to avoid detection. They still smell like people, mixed with stinky stuff. I'll skip the details on what they use.

My suggestion would be that anyone placing trail cameras should use gloves and mask their scent when they place their cameras. A better idea would be a trail camera that had a timer and didn't make noise when it took pictures. Maybe then they will be more successful in their search. It's just a matter of being at the right place at the right time.

As a note to the serious research enthusiasts, I have reviewed over 1000 creatures that were active during the daytime hours. I would say only one in one hundred are lying down. The ones I saw lying down are primarily moms in a nesting area with their young. Young ones appear active at play during the day. Moms are traveling down the trails during the daylight with their cubs in tow. Males are seen carrying food or materials back to the group during the daylight. There is a lot of daytime activity going on. I have no nighttime activity to compare it to, but the analyses of the digital images I have seen lead me to believe that the daylight hours have much Bigfoot activity.

Maybe they are active at night as well or maybe active at night when the moon is full. We can see better at night during a full moon, and animals are affected by the moon just like people. A bright moon gives them enough sight to go out and raid a farm field or steal into someone's yard to snatch colorful small objects. The full moon would also give them an edge to hunt and pounce upon other animals that are roaming around as well.

SMARTER THAN A BEAR

I research some more general animal traits, and think the TV show didn't quite do their research correctly. I know, it's just entertainment, right? But is it something more? What is real and what is just for show? On the internet I see lots of prints and some sightings and pictures. I check out existing pictures, which are blurry and not very definitive. Do good pictures exist?

According to the news sources, they are now attaching cameras to helium balloons, and sending up drones to get treetop views. Maybe they will get some decent footage if they look in the right spot. I don't have those types of resources. I don't get grants, or funding, or have a production budget that lets me buy expensive toys to send aloft or strap onto random trees.

So where can I find something big and scary in the bushes all from the comfort of my cushy couch? I check the internet, of course. I find lots of crap, but hardly any substance or hard evidence. I watch a few more searching type episodes. Someone uses a glider with a camera attached. Lots of area is covered to see a big hairy creature in the woods. I guess it should work if they are not hiding under some trees or in some scrub brush.

I think about tethering a weather balloon to an infrared camera? That would be kind of cool. I would have to devise some fins or stabilizers to hold it in one direction. I wouldn't want it to be spinning in the wind. Next I priced out renting an infrared camera. Nope, I have to skip that! They are still expensive to rent. Way out of my spending range. I'm still sticking to my belief that any animals should be visible in the daytime…maybe even moving about, because they can't see any better than me at night. But where are they?

I had a nagging question. Why aren't more of them hit by cars? I had a hunch. Later I verified that my hunch was correct by sitting quietly along a rural road. Why don't you see them crossing the road? Because they can hear a vehicle coming and so they just hide and wait. If you sit quietly by the side of the road you too can hear approaching vehicles just like they can, and as they pass you can proceed. And they can hide like this right under your nose. If you see one from a four wheeler I would think you are damned lucky. They heard you but ignored the noise by being distracted. Aren't you lucky? You found the dumb one.

I think they sleep at night and not in the daytime. During the daylight they are seen playing and walking and hunting and gathering. They sit quietly on a ledge overlooking a valley and spot you coming into their valley a mile or more before you get there. There are lots of scenes like this evident on the digital map. They are creatures of habit. And I'm sure that they have their favorite spots that they use to hide. You just have to be smarter than them to find that spot. And you need a computer with a digital map to figure it all out.

HOW MANY DOES IT TAKE

Many shows that air on TV identify Bigfoot as one creature that transits through the mountains and causes people to be startled or baffled when they accidentally cross paths. For entertainment purposes, this justifies travel to exotic places and a diverse assignment. If they took their cameras into the scrub brush behind the movie studio, it may get boring. At least they are making the general population aware that these creatures are a possibility anywhere.

A cursory review of the sightings blogs implies that there is more than one Bigfoot type creature in any given area, since the size, description and hair color reported by the witnesses differs. Some sites claim Bigfoot travels across mountain ranges and across states. There is no evidence of nomadic activity. There are enough creatures in each state to justify an occasional sighting. I have documented more than fifty in a five mile radius in most states.

There is a scientific probability number for a community to self-populate and continue to exist. The estimate given is between 3000 and 6000 strong, and that is the minimum. A cursory comparison of known primate studies reveals that any group must be at least 30 strong with males and females of reproduction age to maintain a presence in a given area. If you see one, there is obviously an active population close by.

Evidence further suggests that they must be reproducing strongly enough to at least maintain a viable population, since sightings have continued longer than any known animal's life span. Historically, sightings have been documented for hundreds of years. Logically, they are not the same creatures being seen today. An actual count of the Bigfoot population may exceed the suggested minimum. My research sampled one area of one forest in each state. The location chosen was purely random. The only criteria was that the area should be off the beaten path. The only exception to this criteria was my present home state of Virginia. In Virginia, I have located over 500 within a half hour drive, or roughly within a 60 mile commuting radius.

Mathematically speaking, my research of five square miles of each state showing 50 creatures each multiplied by the tenfold sampling results of the commuting radius raises the probability of a combined population in the range of 300,000 to 600,000. The variables are plentiful food and water source availability, and a habitat zone relatively safe from contact with predators. Since my research did not uncover all creatures in the commuting radius, and it was a baseline statistical sample, the final tally may be even higher..

As a note for the bean counters, I count three times as many babies in my research as I see adults. My research so far reveals an increase of babies per female in the last few years (2007 to 2015). Most females spotted with siblings in tow. Excluding predatory actions of wolves or bears reducing their overall number, their population seems to be on the increase during this time in my study.

I have also compared four years of activity in one location to look for patterns of travel and movement. What I've seen so far appears to show that very few Bigfoot travel alone. No less than three leave the group on a mission. When traveling to water, the whole family travels together. There is obvious pairing of a male and a female while in travel. Most males remain within vocal range of the female with her young in all cases. When sedentary, several females can be often be found sitting in a central location together while their young play together. Childless couples have been seen away from group activities, but probably return to the group for food or rest. All of these observations were made during daylight hours.

A VIOLENCE DISCLAIMER

Due to the nature of the subject matter you may see violent acts in your searches. You may interpret what you are seeing differently from what I think I see. I leave it to your own discretion to locate or view these acts of aggression. I also respect your decision to not look as appropriate. This is life in the wild. You may see brutal acts against other wild animals. You may see animals with blood on their mouth. You may see animals with wounds from fights with other animals. You may see animals eating other animals. You may also see cohabitation, both solicited and unsolicited.

These are wild animals behaving as they do in the wild. You are looking at a moment frozen in time when the animals were performing a specific activity or necessity. This is not desirable viewing for the squeamish.

All of these mentioned here are dangerous and are now in the woods. Any of these may attack if provoked. Any of these may surround you if you are alone in the woods. Some may test you or follow you as you travel through the woods. If you intend to go out into the woods, please use the maps to determine your level of safety. It's not what you can see that will hurt you. It is what you didn't see or know that will. Always be aware of your surroundings. I'm not trying to scare you, but I am concerned. I'm just the messenger. You have been properly warned!

Several websites and other groups have attempted to categorize the various sightings into a cohesive grouping by type. I have not found consistency in their delineation. I have captured many images that do not fit snugly into any one of the categories. Where does Moth Man, Dogman, Lizard Man and the Jersey Devil fit into these categories? That is not my call. I'll let the blog radio hosts hash it out among themselves. They are a judgmental group who worship the Patterson Bigfoot footage as a deity. I have used their generalizations as an outline to give you some idea of what you may see.

Bigfoot is the largest predator often referred to as a type 1. It is an oversized primate that can be twice as tall as a human. They walk upright on two legs, but may run on all fours when speed is necessary. They can be male or female, and are covered with hair from head to toe. They prefer cool to cold weather. They hunt in groups and kill for food. They can run and leap rapidly. They are populous in the northern states from coast to coast. There are sparse in the southern belt. They prefer mountain ravines and dense wooded hillsides.

There is a smaller creature referred to as a type 2 that is a downsized version of Bigfoot. While a type 1 is a full 12 foot tall, a type 2 adult is supposedly between 6 and 8 feet tall. It could also be a type 1. It may just be an adolescent and not fully grown. They seem to live in various climates from cold to hot weather regions. They hunt in packs, and pounce on prey from trees above.

Some have speculated that a type 2 has more human features. I do not find this correct. In my observations, the type 1 has more ape like features. The smaller ones appear more chimp-like. And I find it offensive that someone would classify a derivative species of human as a cryptid animal. The people you may see in the woods should not be referred to as a cryptid type. Although they are not civilized people, they are not animals. Anthropologists may decide that they are of a Neanderthal or Cro-Magnon origin. That is their call. These people could possibly be descendants of some wild woods folk. Or they could be crazy people who found it better to live in the wild. We shouldn't judge until we have more facts. They roam the woods wearing animal skins wrapped around their bodies. They wear animal furs as hats on their heads, and keep the animal face and tail attached to the skin. They are hunters and use sticks as weapons. They are still dangerous. These people are smarter than cryptids and appear to be able to construct a form of shelter. They are misidentified largely due to their pelts and fur they wear, which covers most of their body. Their body hair is naturally like humans and are similar to human in facial features. As such, their gait and locomotion will differentiate them from animals. Perhaps since they are historically undocumented they are easier to misidentify. Several times I have spotted a furry creature in the 6-8 foot range and zoomed to find it was a wild man decked out in fur. The eye holes gave it away. Also the chin and mouth are usually exposed. I have noticed waist cinches being worn as well. If you shot one in the woods thinking they were an animal, it would be an ethical problem. Although numerous in the temperate climate, these have been seen as far north as Maine and Alaska.

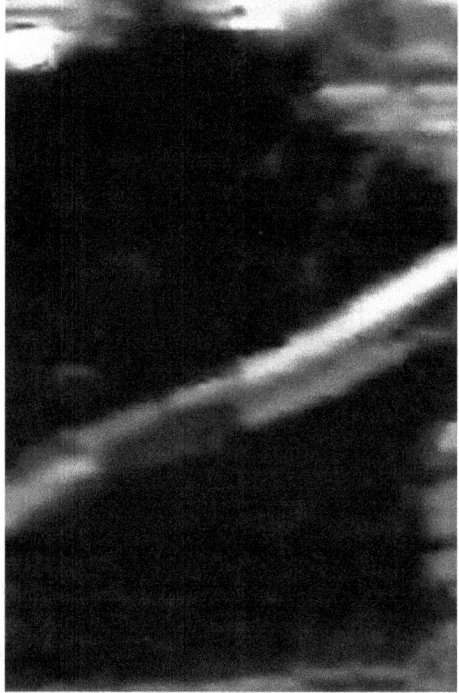

The canine type is referred to as a type 3. These are violent predators with a history of the most violent occurrences. They are barely taller than humans. I have not seen them travel in a pack or nest as a group. They appear to have pointy ears. Most ears I saw were facing back. They appear to have a short snout. Several with a long snout and jowls have been spotted. Gender and age are hard to gauge. They were all seen to walk on two legs. I did not have a four legged sighting. Many sources claim they prefer warm damp climates. They are populous along the Mississippi River and from Texas to Georgia in the southern belt. They are rare further north of the Missouri River. They prefer wooded wetlands and swamp marshes.

There is also a reference to a type 4. There is little information available on this type. I am currently researching geographical location support and physical attributes. These are the little ones. They are supposed to be 2 to 4 feet tall. I've seen some alongside 6 foot tall creatures that were not a classic Bigfoot. There are many shapes and sizes. They are a class of their own, for sure. And they should be considered no less dangerous. I captured their images in a separate file while looking for Bigfoot. I've also seen a video of them on the street in Brazil. The video showed three toes. Maybe this is the three-toed creature? I might have to write another book on just these when I get all the information together.

USING MY RESOURCES

I needed a map to start my search. The one I ended up with was Google Earth. It's free... which is certainly within my price range. I tried Bing first, but Google seemed to have a finer resolution and gets me closer to the subjects. This helped to spot many animals at ground level and also in the trees. I used Google Earth previously a couple of years ago while checking for speed trap areas along the interstate, because radar detectors are illegal in Virginia. It has good definition between shadow and light.

I haven't used Google Earth much since then. I downloaded the program again when I needed to see an overhead view of wooded areas. The difference is now I would be checking in the woods for oversized creatures instead of checking the roads for obvious radar trap areas. OK. So, where do I start? There is a lot of acreage of woods.

As a point picked to start my search I chose a television favorite. I focused on the state of West Virginia, since I have been told that each county apparently has its own monster. I clicked on a random county in West Virginia just over the state line from my present home state of Virginia.

I randomly picked an area not far from where I had visited the Luray Caverns in Virginia not too long ago. I knew there were lots of caves in the area. I figured if I found something interesting in West Virginia, I could plan to take my motorcycle for the two hour drive up through the mountains on an excursion to check it out in person.

Alright then, I thought, let the adventure begin! I tapped down on my touchpad and descended to around 300 feet and started panning a random West Virginia mountainside. I slowly scrolled along and viewed inside and out of the mountainous terrain, up and down the ravines.

The trees were sparse, and the wildlife was less sparse than I had thought.

Minutes turned to into hours. I saw lots of woods, some deer, but no monsters! Damn! It's starting to look like finding a needle in a haystack. I got frustrated and gave up looking after a while once a few hours of hopeless searching had passed. No luck! Bored with looking at trees, I set the laptop aside and turned on the TV.

Destination something-or-other crew travels to Tibet to visit a monastery looking for Yeti. Lots of snow and a monkey scalp. Click. Then I started watching another show where they were searching for a Swamp Ape in Louisiana. Click! Then a light bulb went off. Note to self: They looked similar in appearance. They might be related. A hot squatch and cold squatch could be cousins? Hmmm…

LOCATION...LOCATION...LOCATION

Let me think about this for a minute. So the TV shows take me way up into the mountains. Why? It's a quiet and peaceful place with little intrusions from humans. OK, I'll buy that. After all, it is a mountain monster, right? In another show the swamp monster lives in the quiet and peaceful swamps…away from humans. And I notice the team expedition is never close enough to just make a day trip to visit, like you can when you go visit the zoo. Who wants to backpack in for a few days just to see an animal?

So I need to look again. Back to the computer I go. I spend a couple of hours on different days looking. No luck. I checked lots of random mountain areas at the suggested height above the 2000 foot level.

The shows are right in one aspect. These suckers are sure elusive. What am I missing here? I check the internet and click on some blog accounts. They list old sightings with a general location. Not enough information to map out the area to successfully search. Then I find a site that shows map tags pinpointing where previous sightings have occurred. But the witness statements provided with the map tags are vague. Unreproducible results. Too vague.

It seems that the witnesses are also embarrassed to identify the exact address or even fully identify themselves when they report sightings. This is done for fear of ridicule. In this day and age, that is a crying shame. You are reporting an animal sighting, not a space ship from Mars.

However, from a research point of view, the phrase "along a stretch of interstate 80" is too vague to corroborate. Dead end here…nothing to see folks, unless you like swapping scary stories. I shouldn't talk. I've downloaded quite a few Bigfoot blogs and radio call-ins to listen to as I fall asleep. Which is crazy, since I lay there listening and waiting for how the story ends. Camp sites tore up, people missing, livestock and pets tore apart. Who could go to sleep, once you hear that stuff?

I opened my laptop and searched for some recent activity. Who could sleep with all this stuff going on? I read on further into the last blog website and thought it was odd that all states in the US have reported sightings except for Hawaii. Why? He is not there, or just never been reported? Maybe the information is suppressed to keep the tourist industry happy. I smell a challenge in my slumber-deprived mind. But my motivation kicks on by the questions without answers. Another part to the puzzle. Hawaiian Bigfoot. I'm going to ponder this awhile. But first I have to find a Bigfoot close by.

I go back to the map of West Virginia. I zoom up one random mountainside and follow a ravine back down. Nope. Up another mountainside and then back down into the valley below. There isn't a lot of trees on the mountaintops. I thought this would be easy. There seems to be nothing in the West Virginia Mountains except trees and dirt and rocks.

After a few hours of finding nothing I get bored again. I give up and watch some TV. I watch another episode of a Bigfoot related show. The witness reportedly saw a Bigfoot in the right of way for a gas line construction project. I look at the swaths of trees missing from the side of the hill on the TV. I remember hearing about how big cats and deer can travel easily for miles through an area. Then I next started watching an episode of an encounter where a guy met the TV trackers in a clearing along a power line right of way. Clear cut swaths going up and over the mountain. This started getting my thinker thinking. How do they get in and get out without being seen? The answer is simple. Just follow the lines.

THE POWER LINE CONNECTION

I remember seeing a cougar once in New Jersey. It was around 4am in a rural area where the corn fields met the woods. He only hit the road about three times before he was completely across. He crossed the road under the power lines. Officially there are no cougars or wildcats in New Jersey.

The Division of Fish and Game web site was not helpful. So I asked some local hunters I knew. They all said they don't officially exist in the area, but they all said they have seen at least one while out hunting. They say the big cats follow the game animals as they travel from food source to food source along the power lines. It just made sense.

I pull out the laptop and go back to the map after the show is over. I locate and follow along some West Virginia power lines as they wander over and through the mountainous area. Looking…Looking. Oh, cool. I found a cave. That's something different. I continue scrolling through a valley and scroll across to follow the brush line in the brush dense ravine. I'm scrolling along through the ravine looking at trees and shrubs and more trees and bingo… A monkey!

I must have stared at it for like 10 minutes. I was trying to figure out what else it could possibly be. Was it a tree? Nope. Bear? Nope. I think I found…what? How about a loose escapee from a local zoo? I clicked the compass on the upper right of the screen to rotate the scene. I moved it around to view it at some different angles. It sure as hell looks just like a monkey. It is a rather huge one, at that. It took a while to agree with my brain that it was what I thought I saw. Undoubtedly, it was a big monkey. I tagged it with a map pin so that I could find it again.

Then when I composed myself, I took a deep breath and started cruising slowly up the same ravine from this big monkey and found... even more monkeys! OK...WTF. I'm stoked now. I examined each one by moving closer and moving away to figure out what each one was doing. I tagged each of them with a map pin, as I wanted to find them again. I took another deep breath, and scrolled slowly up the ravine all the way to the top. OK. Done. That was all there was. Then I checked the other side of the mountain. Nope. No more monkeys.

Next I tried the next ravine over from the top to the bottom. No monkeys were found there either. OK, let's figure this out, I thought. I went back and checked out all the monkeys I saw so far. So... the monkeys seemed to be grouped together in the same general vicinity, the brush heavy ravine. And all were doing separate busy activities. One is even carrying a log. One is just sunbathing. Why is there only one ravine with all this activity? Is this the secret Bigfoot location in the West Virginian Mountains? Did I find the secret location everyone is looking for?

CLOSER THAN YOU THINK

One day at work I told my boss that I had spotted some unidentified creatures on my computer while viewing the mountains of West Virginia. I told him that the creatures I saw weren't bears, and they looked just like big monkeys. He said "Oh, it sounds like you saw Bigfoot, huh?" He suggested I talk to a boss on another shift who claims he had a Bigfoot in his back yard. But wait…I thought. How could that be? He doesn't even live in the mountains. He lives surrounded by farmland just off a river. He must be mistaking something else he saw for a Bigfoot.

I made it a point to talk to him later that week, and I told him what I saw in the mountains. He seemed genuinely interested. Then I asked him about his encounter. He told me that he had a family of them living in the woods behind his house. He had someone check out his property with trail cameras and he saw a whole family of them back there. He showed me a hair sample analysis that determined to be of an unknown species. He told me that they liked peanut butter, and could even open the jar. Wow.

I wanted to check his area out to see if I could spot one. So after work I went back home, opened my laptop, and checked on Google Earth to look behind his property and see what I could see.

Here in Virginia, they cut huge swaths of old growth forest and then replant new trees under some guise of conservation efforts to reap a crap ton of money for old growth lumber. The replanted pine tree areas look like rows upon rows in an orchard when viewed from above. These replanted areas are what I refer to as new growth areas. Behind the bosses house the trees are large and old. This is called an old growth area.

The background I received was that here was some homesteading done on this property during the Civil War.

Today nothing remains of the houses except the footings. The acreage is presently leased to a hunting club and is off limits to others (meaning me) without permission. There is only one dirt road that goes through the woods and ends at the river. But I could check it out without trespassing. I fired up my map and headed over into the area.

While checking the map in the old growth area at the edge of the fields behind the boss's property I noticed a clearly defined path snaking through the woods. I zoomed in on the map for a closer look to check it out. The path went from the farmer's field directly to the stream. Since the path wasn't big enough or wide enough for a four wheeler, I figured it was either a farm path to an old secret fishing hole, an old trail to run irrigation line, or a well-established game trail.

I checked out an area further down along the field and I found the dirt access road. The boss had mentioned that the dirt road went from his property all the way down to the river. But I also saw another path. This one ran parallel to the dirt road. I thought that was odd. Why would a path parallel a clear and available dirt road? Was this an old trail before the road was made? Logically it wouldn't be a game trail. Almost all game trails I've seen in the woods intersect roads, not parallel them.

Why would a parallel path exist when a passable route is readily available? The most logical conclusion I could think of was that whoever or whatever made the path intended travel the same direction without being seen from the road. This was starting to get a little eerie.

THE PATHS BEHIND HOUSES

After my initial discovery, I noticed more of these distinct paths through the old growth woods. I started marking them using the Google Earth feature that lets you draw on the map and then save the markup for a reference. Many paths I saw went pretty much directly from a water source to a farm field. Oops! There goes my secret fishing hole trail theory!

Some paths went parallel to farm fields and others were parallel to back yards of houses. Doesn't this seem really odd? I thought so. My first reaction was that maybe these trails were made by something or someone used to travel through the woods to observe the farm fields or back yards covertly.

My second impression was that the paths could be used as needed to be an avenue of a quick escape. From the air looking down at the map, the path seemed to have no underbrush along the corridor and must be heavily travelled. The path beyond the back yards bothered me more than the path alongside the fields. Was the path behind the houses made by wild kids playing in the neighborhood? Or maybe it was some creepy guy checking on his neighbors?

I noted that the back of the yards didn't have fences. There were no outbuildings or structures that encroached or met along the pathway. Would deer make paths parallel to property lines? If there were fences, I could understand deer using a path to get around the fencing. As I searched for comparison properties, I noticed that there were similar lanes in other areas.

After reading some of Dian Fosse's primate studies on primate behavior I came up with a theory. I think that some people are being watched in their own back yards. And the actions in the field are being monitored while waiting for crops to arrive. The more I looked for these types of trails in different rural areas the more trails I found. I identified and marked up the distinct paths between food source, water source and nesting areas as I researched this development.

Later I surmised from all the patterns that all the groups of Bigfoot type creatures I was studying first establish and then continuously use a defined path. It starts at their nesting area and proceeds outward to a known food source and a known water source.

I also found that some groups living closest to humans have beaten a monitoring lane through the woods. This lane runs parallel behind several residential housing areas. The housing areas that have paths seem to be newer homes on old growth properties. The homes might have been built and encroached the Bigfoot territory after the creatures had established area first.

Apparently Bigfoot didn't move away just because the housing was built. They were still in the area, just keeping better tabs on their neighbors.

RATHER UNUSUAL BEHAVIOR

I rarely find one creature hanging out alone. After I spot one I can find another normally within 50 yards of the first. Normally I find a male and female together, or in very close proximity to each other. Most times females are with several babies. Many I have seen have four or more hanging on to their mother as they travel. The smallest babies appear to be carried by the female on her head. Don't ask me why. That answer will have to wait for someone who has the time to analyze this unusual behavior.

There are many times I didn't save a picture because there are many animals clustered together, making identification difficult. The male is usually found cruising or just wandering idly in the vicinity close by if the group is stationary. He has been seen carrying the young ones sometimes when they are traveling. The male gives the impression that he, as males do in many species, provides protection and security for the mom and babies.

As in other monogamous mammals, a male and a female can occasionally be seen pairing off and moving away from the group to a quiet space with no other noticeable creature activity. I think it may be for privacy. Do not for a minute believe that when you spot one, that it is alone. Even though on first appearance the couple seems to be alone in the woods, scrolling upward to a larger view shows that they are from a group (at least 30) that is active within a half mile of their seclusion spot. The group is easily within calling distance. When you find the couple you will also find the local group in that particular area of the woods.

I have seen a group population divided into two groups due to construction of a new roadway. I don't know if a couple with child would voluntarily leave the security of the group to begin a new group on their own. I have seen males working on nests and play areas. The male seems to be the builder. The female may provide the bedding material to finish the nest. The female sits around the nest doing something. The females sit around the play area doing something too. I just don't know what. I can't tell if females are plucking leaves or not. The male brings the lumber. He is definitely the alpha. I see that.

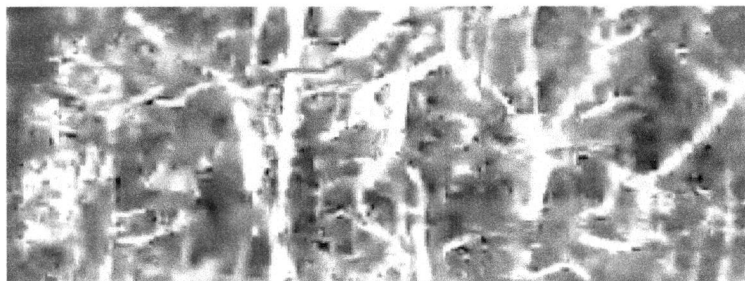

Contrary to popular belief, the groups I have found are not only in the mountains, or at the higher elevations. They have chosen quiet sides of a hillside, or chosen a side of the next mountain over from civilization. They have established and maintain play zones and nesting areas. Some have taken over abandoned buildings and sheds to protect them from the weather. Most are located where humans do not normally go.

They have designated spotters to warn them of approaching danger. They have group security roaming outside of the play zones, where the moms and babies can watch their little ones play safely. Some are located close to human housing areas. These have been displaced by clear cut of the woods and have moved from their original nesting areas. They take safety precautions to prevent surprise visits by intruders. They discretely monitor the adjacent human housing areas. They have established spy trails to observe their human neighbors in secret and can discretely escape before detection.

We are talking wild animals here, but there are patterns exhibited in their behavior. And it's all recorded and frozen in time on a digital map plate for anyone to analyze. Sometimes they are very close to us. I was surprised that so many live near my house. I thought I would have to drive a long distance to go looking for them.

What I found was three major concentrations within a 30 minute drive. Almost all of the pictures in this book were taken within 15 minutes from my house. I've seen active nesting areas as close as 200 yards from a paved rural road with houses scattered nearby. Some I drove by to visit. I couldn't legally enter the woods because it was privately owned and posted. Get permission before you enter someone else's property. I don't know who put up the No Trespassing signs, but it was probably because of hunters causing problems. Apparently living on posted property benefits the creatures who live there as well as keeps out any avid Bigfoot explorers. But you can still use a zoom and get some half decent pictures.

GET IN THE ZONE

I have established that the group provides its own security. That is evident from the community scenes. It must have been developed for the safety of their community. I don't know how it was determined that this was important, or if it just evolved as a best method. It is evident of a group effort to have designated point guards in the edges of fields, spotters along the roadways, and watchers near the housing.

Some sit within 50 feet alongside rural roads and interstates. Are they amazed at the traffic zooming by, or just waiting for some vehicle to stop and present a danger to the group? Some sit at the corners of farm fields, as if keeping watch on the machinery and movement in the field. Some stand watch along the paths and dirt roads entering their fortress. Are they the bouncers or just the early alarm? There isn't enough information yet. But I see some intelligent group behavior that I wouldn't have expected from animals.

I know I'm giving these animals a lot of credit if what I am seeing is correct. The watchers are stationed forward of the group about a half mile or less at a strategic location. I say it is a strategic point because I was in the military, and I would station someone there if I wanted someone on point to alert my group. It is a strategic move to cover the entrance point. I don't know how they know it was a good location. It's a good hiding spot with effective cover that has a wide field of view to keep an eye on any movement from someone or something coming in.

I emphasize this because if they are intelligent enough to have an early warning system in place, then they are smart enough to rapidly vacate if infiltration by humans is imminent. They could be clearly a mile or more further into the forest before you even get out of your truck. I don't yet know how they would communicate this alarm to the rest of the group. Is the wood knocking or howling used as part in this alarm? I don't think so. That's only on TV. I believe that the spotter who sees a hunter or tractor runs back to alert the others.

Now I know I have seen many creatures just sitting alongside of the road. I have taken their picture doing just that. Perhaps they are amazed or amused by the different types of vehicles that whizz on by. But I haven't seen one sitting by the road without a group somewhere behind. And I haven't seen a loner just wandering around someone's garage. They all seem to have a communal purpose. They all have a job or a task.

I'm not sure that primates in captivity demonstrate this capacity. I can't find this type of behavior noted in any primate research. I just know what I see. And I am telling you. But if you don't believe what I am saying, don't be an armchair quarterback. You don't have to believe me. You have the resources available on your own computer to look at the same things I see and decide for yourself.

One scene that made me think that writing this down and letting others know was a good idea. A tractor trailer was pulled to the side of Interstate 95 here in central Virginia, and a Bigfoot watcher was on the berm next to the roadway looking down on the semi. This is a scary scene. Think about it.

BLONDES, BRUNETTES AND REDHEADS

There seems to be at six solid hair colors: Black, Brown, Tan, Red, White and Gray. There are also two-toned ones. I have seen examples of black ones with a white face and belly, and dark brown ones with a tan face and belly. There are also spotted or mottled ones with two or more hair colors. Black, white and brown species with the pointed nose and pointed ears are all over.

I haven't figured out if there are other differences in each species beside their hair color. The features vary, but so do human features. I guess once someone gets some grant money to obtain solid anthropological data on these species, we can find out if there is a pure breed living among all these variants. There may be some crossbreeding going on due to geographical isolation.

There seems to be more than the four types as most experts claim. As I stated earlier, I think the predominant ones across the globe are the primate types and secondary are the canine types. There appears to be at least two sizes of primates and two sizes of canines. There are also others that don't fit snugly into either category. As my research continues I will try to separate all the types into more specific categories. There is a lot still to learn about this other community that inhabits the woodlands and swamps.

I have seen the various combinations of hair colors and all species variants together in one area as a group. They appear to coexist together peacefully, as they are lounging, playing or traveling side by side. I have yet to see any tan babies yet. I don't know if they just blend with the pixilation of the map program and are hard to see, or if they have a recessive gene that is not as prevalent in the young.

Every group of approximately 30 adults in a given area has approximately 100 babies or juveniles visible.

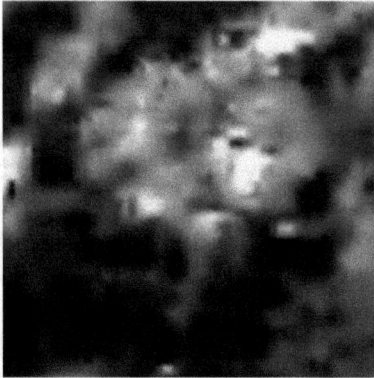

Consider that if one third of the babies fall victim to hawks or accidental death, the number that will survive to grow through adolescence into adulthood is still greater in number than the current population of breeding adults. This leads me to believe that the population of these creatures is still on the upswing.

On the babies I saw so far, most are black or reddish brown. Some have dark pigmentation with dark hair and some have light tan pigmentation with reddish brown hair. I don't know if the hair color changes as they get older, making the dark brown from the reddish brown. I'm guessing that the Gray ones must be the elderly. Grandma and grandpa, I think. Gray ones seem haggard and ugly, with matted straggly hair and sunken eyes. They have flowing mustache and long beards, and their crown is not as pronounced. I can't see the ears for the hair. I've only seen one short gray, which may have been a really old one.

Again, I have nothing to compare their aging process to, except maybe using existing primate research. I'm not sure how old they are when I see them, or what their life span actually is. Does the hair turn gray in all the hair colors, or is it prevalent in only one? I know my domestic animals get gray hair, but I haven't seen an animal turn completely gray. We can only speculate their age and life span until we get more information. I found one small white albino baby so far with pointed ears and red eyes. The albino seems to be as rare to these creatures as it is in humans.

As far as the largest primate types I've seen, it seems the largest ones are the black haired males. They are the ones that look like King Kong. They are also the hardest to photograph. While the tan and brown primate types look like capuchin features, the black ones look like old world gorillas. You will know one when you see one. Most of the young ones look like a chimp type primate, with a protruding smooth mouth area and wide set mouth. They have fine hair with big oversized ears. No long chin hair or lip hair. And they are cute, as a baby monkey would be. But be careful if you find a baby alone in the woods nestled near a tree because the mama is always nearby. That's a survival fact you should already know.

Normally I spot the mom first, for obvious reasons, and then I see and identify where all her little ones are. Most are normally seen being carried by the mama as they move down the path through the woods. The cubs seem to hang on their mama's back and peer over her shoulder during travel. If the travel is urgent enough, the mama will scoop up her youth and carry them under her arms. Maybe they are in the state of alarm, and need to relocate to a safer area. The adults seem to move their young to safety swiftly, just like any parent would.

Other times whole families can be viewed traveling together down a path with the young ones at their feet. This seems to be a casual stroll without danger present. Maybe they are headed to the watering hole. More recently I noted that not all cubs are necessarily the same fur color as the mama. I don't know if this is mixing breeds, or if they are like rabbits that have variations of color with successive births.

Not all babies can be easily identified due to the fact that they are clinging to the mama with their faces away from the viewer. The youth that ride on the mama's back peer over her shoulder and their face can be seen clearly, since they are facing the same way as the mom.

I haven't seen a canine type riding on their mama yet. Maybe they raise their young differently. Maybe there is a litter of them stashed under a tree somewhere. There is a difference in maternal behavior to note.

PLAYING ON THE MONKEY BARS

Some of the playful scenes I see on the digital maps remind me of a visit to the zoo. I have tagged these play areas and hope to explore them at a later date for physical evidence. Unlike the nest, which is made of branches crossed over each other to protect young ones from predators, these areas seem more sparsely arranged: six or more long tree trunks snapped and set in crooks of another tree about four to six feet high. Some have bent over saplings held down by cross trunks and they are poked into the ground with no root area present.

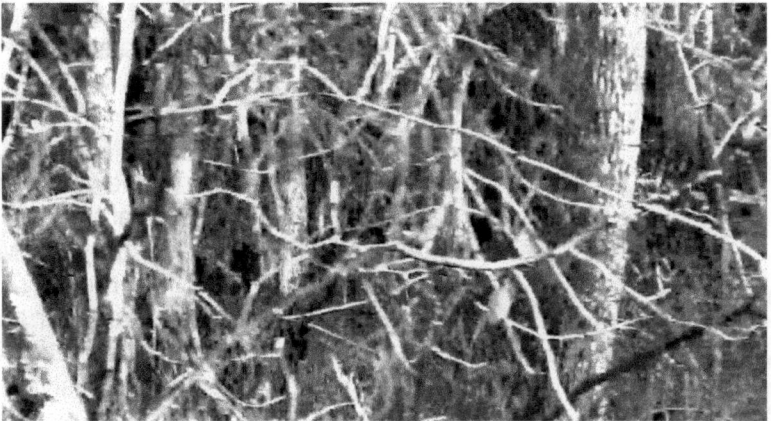

These configurations provide a variable height climbing and playing area for the young ones. The moms sit around the play area with their babies and watch their young ones interact and play with others. The young ones swing, climb, straddle and hang on the "monkey bars" made just for them. The babies crawl around at their mom's feet while the older ones play. Being an outsider, I get the feeling that this is like watching a primate version of a daycare center. It is surreal for wild animal behavior.

I use the term young and adolescent without knowing for sure the ages of the creatures. I'm just trying to give you an idea of the general age of the participant, so that you know what is going on. If the animal is a medium height of three or four feet tall, I use cub and young interchangeably. I know cub may be associated with bears, but I don't know of a more proper term for them until they are identified.

The medium height is roughly comparable to a youth of six to twelve years old in human age. The small ones less than 3 feet tall or the ones sitting in moms lap or riding on her shoulders or head, I call a baby, a tyke or little one. It could be a newborn to a two year old. We don't know the average birth weight yet, so it is only an educated guess based on the observed behavior. If someone sees a birth as it is happening, then we will know.

Once we get rolling on the identification process of these species, we can establish a standard. I've just used three sizes: small, medium and large. I've been using the ruler tool provided on Google Earth to measure their approximate size. It is not as accurate as I had hoped, because tire tracks seem to be ten foot wide, and I know that is not correct.

For some reason, ten foot is not an uncommon height for a mature looking adult. Some adults are 12 foot tall. I have measured quite a few here in Virginia that were that tall. The females are noticeably smaller, but still larger than humans.

I know if I get too close to one, I'm going to be intimidated by its size. The TV shows say eight foot is common. A Bigfoot at 8 feet tall seems more like an adolescent size. Or if you go by type, they may be a type 2. Maybe they are like deer, and have evolved based on their surroundings.

There seems to be no difference in size among the different areas I have researched so far. The ones in Washington and Oregon seem the same as the ones here in Virginia. But the tools to measure and verify are not as accurate as we need.

We just don't have good information to make anything more than an educated guess. It's like guessing how long a unicorn horn is. There just isn't enough concrete data.

NESTING LIKE A BIRD

I first made the mistake when I started searching of tagging tree branch piles on the map as bone piles. I saw big skulls under big piles of branches and thought I had found a bone yard. I was so pumped! I now had a destination to explore for evidence. I could walk right into the woods and pick up one of the Bigfoot skulls. Cool.

I decided I should take a measurement of the various skull sizes I saw in the pile under the branch pile. When I measured them using the ruler tool, they seemed big enough to be a Bigfoot creature. They were much too large to be a human and not shaped like a horse or deer skull would be. I also saw that there was an active community of Bigfoot type creatures roaming about nearby.

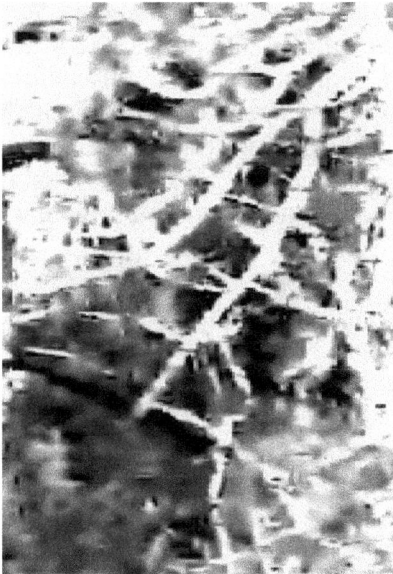

OK so this was my plan: Once I got out into the woods and went to the grid location I would approach the pile of bones noisily. The Bigfoot would cautiously step away into the undergrowth while I poked through their recently deceased relatives bone pile. Cool plan, huh? They would passively watch me take their relatives bones without any howling or screaming or throwing rocks or giving up their hiding spot. Yeah, right!

They say Bigfoot is an elusive creature, or so I hear. And so are Bigfoot bones. I located on the map some large bones in a closer area, jumbled on the side of a steep slope. There was a road that hugged the bottom of the hill slope. I saw where the road comes really close to the bone pile location. Now I didn't have to lug the bones too far to get them out of the woods.

Why anyone hasn't discovered a pile of Bigfoot bones yet I don't know, I thought. I'm seeing bone piles in every Bigfoot group location, placed conveniently in the middle of the group like a local Bigfoot cemetery. It's Bigfoot bone hunting treasure time!

Then all of a sudden the light bulb came on. While I stared at the map of the bright white bones a dreaded reality sunk in. I think I know why the bones are massed together. Let me rethink this again.

Reevaluating this situation, I used my cursor and ascended above the slope. I zoomed next to the earlier bone site I had previously tagged. Using the ruler tool I measured the bone lengths at the bone site. Some were the right length, but some of the bleach white lengths were too long to be Bigfoot bones. These weren't bone piles I was looking at. Instead these are active Bigfoot nests! What I thought were bones and skulls were instead live snoozing animals! Side by side and cuddled together, their heads on a log. Damn! They aren't even dead yet. I'm sure glad I didn't just barge in to their lair thinking it was just a pile of bones! That would have been rough. Whew!

When I began visiting the nest sites alongside the railroad I was disappointed. Nobody was home. I saw just a bunch of flattened grasses or else piles of pine needles. No noticeable smell, and of course no bones. I was disappointed. I took some digital pictures of the empty nests just to show that I was there.

Most had one fallen tree as the support beam with smaller trees poked into the ground and leaning on the support beam tree. Six to eight foot long trees about 6 to 8 inches around were uprooted and the dirt was knocked off.

They were propped against the anchor beam tree at odd angles.

The uprooted trees came from somewhere else, because there were no stump holes or any kind of shallow hollow in the vicinity. I checked the surrounding area about 200 feet around the nest and found no ground disturbance. I don't know how far they were brought before they ended up here.

Some of the nests I visited that day in the woods had vines growing between the branches and were intertwined in the overhead, providing a pleasing garden-like setting. I was on my hands and knees in a Bigfoot nest. I was tempted to lie on my back to see the view, but I changed my mind. I didn't want to get too comfortable. Or become vulnerable.

I returned home and looked at the map again, to see where I had traveled. I realized that the nests I visited and photographed in the field were not the nests that I originally saw the animals huddled in. They were on the map as well, but nobody was home on that day either. I'll plan to visit the occupied nests on my next outing to see if I can find some stinky ones. Or maybe I'll find an active one. Empty or full when I get there will be my surprise.

BIGFOOT HAS SOME PETS

I have seen small canine and feline domestic looking animals hanging around with groups of Bigfoot. Some are asleep beside them, and some are sitting on top of them. Are they their pets? Are they little Bigfoot babies that look like small furry animals? If they are canine type Bigfoot, they are not with a canine mama. They look more like short haired domestic pets.

I'm not sure that stray cats or dogs roaming the woods would buddy up to Bigfoot as a companion unless they were hungry. For all I know, the ones lying next to the creatures could be asleep or may be dead. The cats I see sitting on top of the Bigfoot creatures are still obviously living. Is this where all the stray kittens go when they go off into the woods?

I saw a cat looking animal draped on the head of a female Bigfoot with its paws hanging down. There was a baby Bigfoot nestled above the cat. That was weird. Then I saw a bird looking thing on its head. That was fashionable, I guess. I can't easily explain away what I saw. This isn't a Dr. Seuss land. It is woodland creatures in the woods wearing cats on their heads like Daniel Boone. Crazy, isn't it? I know a bird and a cat do not stack well. My guess is that the birds seen may be an acquired adornment. This might be a learned behavior from watching humans going to church? I've also seen human looking baby faces on a few heads. That doesn't make sense either. Maybe the creatures stole doll toys or yard ornaments from someone's back yard. Now they wear these things as an accessory. I just can't logically explain some of the weird things I am seeing.

Was the Bigfoot baby tucked into the cat fur used for warmth as a blanket? Maybe it is used as protective cover from the hawks overhead? Are the domestic looking dogs I see standing next to the Bigfoot their beloved companion, some type of pet, or are they just being kept around until they become a meal? Does a domestic animal even know what a squatch will do to them if the squatch gets hungry?

Creatures having pets is awfully confusing. It doesn't make sense. I'm not sure of the purpose or the intelligence level of these creatures to begin with. This just makes matters worse. I can make a slightly reasonable assumption, but no formidable conclusion. I just know that, dead or alive, these domestic animals that we associate with and love as one of our own appear to be actively involved in the Bigfoot creature's circle. Why they are present, and if they are being treated well, I can only speculate.

The more I see during this research the less I can explain. This is why I want to share this with you. I need you to see some of these things. You can see everything that I see. Maybe you can help solve some of the missing parts of this puzzle. You will be working off the same sheet music as me. You too will have your first impression like I had mine. You might just come up with a better answer. All this information is not on the internet. And the answers aren't anywhere on the internet. I checked.

DANCING WITH WOLVES

I have seen packs of wolves very close to Bigfoot activities. They have even share lunch together sometimes. I have seen single wolves hovering very close to a group of Bigfoot. They seem to coexist in the same vicinity, but I don't get the impression that wolves are their pets. Conversely, I've also seen dead wolves being carried by Bigfoot. My first impression was that this dead wolf may be Bigfoot's lunch.

Wolves can be beneficial neighbors to Bigfoot as a first alert warning system, as they howl when they hear noise. The first time I saw Bigfoot interact with wolves was a pack of wolves surrounding a Bigfoot lying on the ground. The Bigfoot was on its back with arms and feet spread. And the wolves appeared to be tugging at it. I couldn't make out the expression on the Bigfoot to determine if it was still alive. It may have been playing. Or it may have been dead. My first impression was horror: A lone Bigfoot being attacked by a pack of wolves. Not a pretty sight.

This was the also the first scene of violence I found. It was definitely not the only one. After staring at it for a very long time, and trying to decide what was going on, I tagged it on my map to find it later. I also added it to my list of places I want to check for Bigfoot bones. I will also definitely be packing some firepower when I visit this site, of course. Just in case.

Now bears are another story. Are they the junkyard dogs of the woods? They patrol the woods and scare off the strangers. They have a defined role in this forest community. I have seen bears in close proximity of 50 foot or less from active Bigfoot groups and their nesting sites, but rarely inside the camp of the Bigfoot. Once so far I did see a female bear with cubs sitting very close to a female Bigfoot with her cubs. Maybe it was a play date. I don't know if it is maternal instinct that prevents violence between them. So far this was the only time Bigfoot and bear were sitting together.

Maybe the males are the ones that cannot get along together. I never saw male bears and Bigfoot together. Most male bears I notice seem to be roaming aimlessly near the Bigfoot group I was documenting. Unless he is patrolling, why would he be active without a purpose? Unlike Bigfoot creatures, most bears I saw were males. They were traveling alone or wandering through the woods solo. Hungry strays, perhaps? The bears in close proximity to a group of Bigfoot may possibly share the same food source or wait for leftover spoils. I never saw them eating together, and the male bears don't breach the Bigfoot group, so I can't figure out the connection.

The female bears I have seen so far seem to be preoccupied with their babies in a stationary location. I haven't seen a traveling female bear carrying her bear cubs. The female Bigfoot has been seen often traveling through the woods with young ones in tow during the daytime. They appear much more mobile than the bears. Maybe that is why you are more likely to spot a bear first.

JUST FOLLOW THE FOOD

While fish and small game seem likely, there is plenty to eat if you know where to look. Think of yourself as lost in the woods. What would you eat?

Fresh stalks, berries, nuts and fruit. They probably have the same diet. Locally the groups I have seen have been close to farm fields. One I scouted nearby has corn fields to the east and soybean fields to the south. Seasonally, it's a plentiful harvest fresh for the picking.

The tractors rarely come out at night, so night time is the best time to raid the fields. Also to note there is always a water source nearby, and the path goes directly down to it. After reading more on primate studies, I found out that primates do eat meat, which is roughly 30% of their diet. I think that meat has been consumed way too much in my research to be 30% of their diet. I think meat is their primary source of protein.

Other sources agree and state these creatures to be primarily carnivorous by evidence of their canine teeth. I am trying to get better pictures of them with their mouths open. I saw one that looked like a double row of teeth. This has been speculated on websites and blogs by others.

A sidebar note is that September and October are the heaviest meat consumption times, according to sources. Maybe the protein is used for fat storage over the winter. Or maybe the plentiful field harvest in autumn and they need to supplement their diet in winter with game animals as a food source until spring brings new fruit.

Most of my research was viewed in April. The crops aren't ready. The deer were available as a food source. Deer seem to be plentiful and easily available within short distances from many of the groups I have found. And there is a lot of deer seen being devoured on the days the digital maps were taken. April is too early for fruit to bear, and farms have no protein available in the fields. April is also a bad month to be a deer.

Deer are ambushed and taken down by a group of four or five adult males. During the tackle one will break the back or neck and it will end the struggle. Young adults can be seen running alongside the takedown. They also participate in the event.

IT IS ONLY NATURAL

I started on the assumption that the male is larger than the female. It wasn't to my surprise that I was correct. I took some information stated as fact from the Bigfoot shows on TV and verified. This was one of the few facts that were correct from the various television shows I saw.

So here I am zooming around the area to find more on the map. I saw a tan head sticking out in the forest so I descended down and zoomed in on one... and OMG it had breasts! And they were big ones. Yup, that's a female, all right! I wonder if she knew her picture was being taken.

Not since reading National Geographic magazines in the school library as a child have I felt so awkward. But I was researching, so it was OK. While the viewing level does pixilate if you zoom too much, I can safely presume this was a female because I know what I see: Bigfoot breasts. For the details you can find out for yourself.

The black haired males have little or no chest hair near their nipples (think King Kong), and appear buff. The lighter haired males are shaggier with less muscle definition visible. They may all be built alike, but the furrier males are less buff in appearance.

Now when I tag a file, if the gender is obvious I include a gender identification designator showing the picture as either a male or a female. I don't know if gender will matter at a later date, but I started using a gender code designator if it is known.

Of course I have seen various configurations that could be judged in many ways. Yes, there's the jungle sex. I have seen a female leaning forward with the male pressed up behind her. Maybe he was just helping her keep her balance. I know this is speculative, but the positioning is classic. I saw another female on all fours with a male kneeling behind her. Maybe she had fallen and he was helping her to get up. Maybe this would make a book unto itself, but I will not include these pictures here.

And I saw a couple spooning together in their nest. This was after I discovered what an active nest looked like, of course. Thank goodness I didn't go out poking around in brush piles without knowing what I now know. I still believe that the nest is built to keep babies safe from falcons and eagles while the mother rests. Maybe these couples are newlyweds. But I still think they shouldn't be doing that in front of the baby.

I know this is considered natural behavior, and I'm telling you only so you do not get surprised like I did. I still feel awkward finding and staring at them doing their thing on my computer screen.

ON MIGRATION

I have heard self-proclaimed experts postulate about Bigfoot migration patterns. They speculate that the animals move to higher and lower elevations during certain seasons. That is not what I see. I haven't needed to be present on a mountain over the course of several years to ascertain whether they are here or there. I have studied Google Earth maps dated from the years 2007, 2009, 2011, 2014 and 2015. I also studied different seasons (i.e. Jan, April, July and Oct) from the same year when they were available. Some states have more available research data than others.

Water, shelter and food. All three of these are necessary to sustain a group of Bigfoot in an area. All three elements are within several miles of every group sighting so far. I have noted on my map that the areas of Bigfoot activity have a seasonal food source and a continuous water source located nearby. The location where they prefer to play, sleep and nest is usually a natural windbreak, like a ravine or hollow. They prefer dense grass, thickets or woods, due to its protection from the weather.

They hunt and they gather. They know the location of seasonal fruit and vegetables, and feed on the plentiful supply as it becomes available. They hunt animals when easy food is not in season. This pattern provides small game a nice break during mating season. The hunting would be minimal until after fall harvest, when the easy food disappears. The Bigfoot groups I studied over time in woods and swamps around farmland have sufficient resources to stay within the area

Mountaintops seem to provide no incentive except game animals. Any seen crossing ridges or mountains is experiencing hard times. I have not seen any on the mountaintops, and I have checked many. Maybe those seen at higher elevations are moving away from infringed territory. Valleys and ravines of the mountains are the active locations with a variety of food to choose from. These areas are also more likely locations for shelter from bad weather. Nuts, berries, grasses, grains, and small game are available year round in the folds of the mountain. From the Badlands of Montana to the White Sands of New Mexico, active groups can be seen in the ravines beyond the towns. Plentiful game animals roam these lower levels adjacent to the valleys in most observed areas.

My analysis shows that the same amount of animals continue to frequent a static area over time. In some instances where a manmade border provided a defined tract of active woodlands to give a precise count, an increase in population was noted as time progressed. This leads me to the conclusion all three elements are available for habitat, and that their population is either static or growing.

During my population density studies I identified a group of Bigfoot creatures that had migrated slowly a mile upriver between the years 2007 and 2014. This seemed a little puzzling at first. Located smack dab between farm fields and a river. Why would they want to move?

I learned from a local resident that construction of single family housing occurred a half mile from the group's original location. Finding this piece of the puzzle, I concluded that the group movement was due to a new housing development. The sounds of construction equipment and smells of humans had sent them packing for a quieter knoll further away.

ON AGGRESSION

This is a tricky thing to analyze and report on without causing alarm. Here in the US there are numerous people wandering through the woods all the time. Fortunately most now have cameras available to record events during their hikes and walks through the woods. I know from experience that many newsworthy events have never been successfully recorded.

I have spent a lot of time in the woods as a kid, and spent many weekends in the jungle as an adult. I've never been fearful of the known animals of the woods, but I'm a little uneasy about roaming around unarmed looking for an unpredictable eight foot animal. I hope I can defend myself if I need to, but the speed at which these animals move and can turn events around to an unsafe situation is not predictable.

Of course if I saw a bear cub in the woods I would back off and be very cautious, because I know the momma bear is close by. It's only common sense. And common sense will keep you safe if you have common sense. It's not good to stumble across an animal that has to decide either to fight for territory, or to fight to save their cubs. It's not a good place to be. Back out slowly. You are going to lose.

I know there is violence in primate communities by what I have read and seen. I recently saved a picture of one Bigfoot choking another. Maybe they were just playing. Or maybe not. Maybe the animals mating in the woods were willing participants. Or maybe they were not. Sometimes your first reaction is the correct one.

Animals I have seen overtaken by Bigfoot were taken by a group of them. This is classic primate behavior, and I think that primate behavior is appropriately labeled to all Bigfoot activities. They more than likely dropped from the trees onto the surprised animal below. I don't know if they use a signal to attack. The pack got the drop on them.

You can armchair quarterback any scene you see on Google Earth or Bing all you want. Your gut reaction may be the same as mine. I just know I don't want to be a participant in a scene like that, thank you. Is Bigfoot alone feared in the woods, or are they fearful and only show bravery in numbers? Is the aggression limited to only pack behavior, and not in individual one-on-one confrontation? I'll leave that to the field observers to decide.

My best guess is if you stumble across one, he will leave first. If you stumble across an active nest or a hungry group, good luck. Some groups live precariously close to human housing. You will see this when you take a look. Don't leave your pies on the window sill. And keep an eye on your backyard grill. If they want to get to some good smelling mouthwatering food, who is going to stop them?

BEST DEFENSE

I could not find any information online regarding Bigfoots defense against aggression. I know they throw rocks at intruders to chase them away. Their aim isn't very good, unless they don't have much practice. But do they also use rocks as weapons? Will they bring rocks to a rock fight? How about as a personal defense to feel secure? The reason why these questions came up is that I've noticed some peculiar reaction expressions while analyzing scenes. Some were running with their mouth open. The expression looked like fear. This is Bigfoot, king of the jungle. Running, and afraid.

Another time a Bigfoot was making strange faces while wrestling with another. I couldn't determine from the photo if it was in play or it was defensive in nature. Do they have a group leader? They obviously work together as hunters. They probably work together as gatherers. They select sentries for security. Do they use rocks as personal protection? Does this behavior mirror primates as well?

I found a clue to my questions while on my excursion to see a Bigfoot. While following a freshly beaten trail through the grasses I ended up at a large pond. At the edge of a pond I noticed several bricks, half bricks and small 6" by 6" square stones. They were lying on the left side of the path in the shore grass. These were manmade items. There is no source of bricks close by. Since there is no brick foundation or construction of buildings within 2 miles of the area, I can only presume the bricks were brought here from another location. Unless they came from a rucksack, there were too many for one person to carry. They were not wet or dirty, they were fresh. Who would stack some bricks at the edge of a pond?

Did they run off scared as someone approached or did they just wander off and forgot their protective weapons, I wondered? Maybe it was me who scared them off. Maybe they had taken a swim? I doubled back to a side trail but there was no smell present in the air. There were no other grasses crushed down in any other direction. I looked in the trees that ended at the pond edge. Not here. Where did they go?

I went back to the bricks at the edge of the pond. Nothing recent besides the bricks was here. Someone had put the bricks next to the pond today. It had rained yesterday, and the ground was damp in the morning dew, but the bricks were dry. I picked one up. No hair on it. The brick under a brick was not damp. The bottom of the bricks was not wet. Not even damp like the moist ground.

Later that day, I found more half bricks near the railroad tracks. There are mounds of dirt with tall grasses under the high tension lines that cross the track. I think the mounds were put there to keep vehicles out. These bricks were in an area of flattened grasses on the far side of the track. There were four flattened areas. I am guessing that the bricks may be defensive, stashed there just in case. Again, I can only guess the answer. They seem a little smarter than animals I am used to dealing with.

ABOUT THAT SMELL

These animals have a noticeable smell like a garbage truck. While walking in the woods between a pond and railroad tracks I smelled the smell. I took note that the light breeze was coming from across the swamp. When I scanned the edges I saw something perched on a log dangling something in the water. Maybe cleaning his food, or cleaning crap off his paw? I took a minute to try to figure out what kind of animal it was. It was not huge. It shimmied across the log and started picking sprouts. I picked up my camera to take some video and hit the wrong button. I got pics instead.

The sun reflecting off the water made my subject a shadow in the lens. When I tried to get some video using the telephoto it is shaky. I needed to brace my arm to get a stable image. Now I see why there is not good footage anywhere. I wasn't scared, but my camera shook. I backed away from the ledge and quietly moved fifty or more feet to a better viewing area, but then I couldn't find him again.

I panned the pond, but couldn't find the log anymore from this angle. I guessed that he was done whatever he was doing. I noted that the smell was gone, too. I waited 20 minutes scanning for movement along the bank then I moved on. When I got home I reviewed my footage. I panned my camera right past two Bigfoot standing on the banks watching a Bigfoot cub picking grasses. I didn't even notice them stranding there.

I ended up with only 2 or 3 good seconds of footage. If I had went around the swamp I would have ran into them. I just assumed that they left because I didn't see them any longer. I could have cornered them, or at least trapped the cub on the log. In hindsight, I'm glad I didn't follow up on them. I wasn't armed, and they may not have liked me cornering their cub on a log over the swamp. The next time I go out on an excursion, I think I will take some personal protection. I have seen these Bigfoot creatures pouncing on deer. I don't want to be pounced myself while trying to get some good video footage. Three against one is not good odds. When I'm done with my excursion, I want to leave in one piece.

THE COMMUTERS

So here is the synopsis so far. I proved to myself that these creatures exist. First I tagged the area on a map where they once were. Then I took a trip and saw them in the same location. I want to make several more trips to visit another sighting area close by to confirm that this is not just a fluke of luck. I spent three hours looking for Bigfoot. Some people spend years. Maybe I was just lucky to find the only Bigfoot that exist in Virginia (insert laughter here). Just kidding! There's more. Lots more.

Secondly, while I was in the woods verifying what I saw on the map, I walked some paths that I thought they had made. I've been on lots of deer trails, and made my own trails through the woods. This kind was different. It was a walking trail, with six inch lush grass and covered overhead by trees. It was shady and woodsy smelling. The grass was mashed down but not browned out in a nine or ten inch swath. It was a pleasant path to walk. No debris or fallen limbs. OK, I'm no Crocodile Dundee. When the path came to a stream, I stopped. It wasn't deep, nor was it wide. It was wider than I could jump, though. I opted to go around by land instead of getting my shoes and socks wet. What a wuss.

I followed the mashed grass and saw where the stream bottom was disturbed. There was a footprint but it was underwater. That will never fly as credible evidence. I looked through the camera sight but it wasn't impressive. I also didn't see any reasonable depressions or noticeable distinct tracks on the grassy bank good enough for measuring. Next trip maybe.

And third, I confirmed by an actual count and subsequent density analysis that these creatures are presently living not only in distant forests and remote swamps, but also near human dwellings. I have located their spy trails that parallel dirt roads. I have identified the wooded paths which parallel the back yards of housing developments. I traced their escape routes from these housing areas directly back to their nest. I have been able to identify their primary field food source and their path to their primary water source.

And last, I wanted to see what is grown in those fields that was such a draw to these animals. I drove to the farm field I saw on the map, and parked in a church parking lot next door. The farm is bordered by woods, a swamp and a church. The woods are posted. Another Bigfoot safe haven. The security guy pulled through the church parking lot and was checking me out while I walked to the edge of the field. The field was barren during my first visit. It was not an orchard. It had to be an edible vegetable of some sort. I went back several months later for a follow-up visit. The field was full of soy beans. Interesting. I guess you learn something new every day.

BUNCH OF THIEVES

Secure your property. Don't leave items around in your back yard. These creatures steal loose items from people's yards as observed carrying items away into the woods. I have seen them sitting in the woods with an unusual object on their lap. I have seen one with a shiny ball high up in a tree.

Maybe it becomes a trophy or revered object to prove their trip into the forbidden human zone. Maybe the urge to inspect the item in the safety of the woods is the reason for the theft. Maybe they see someone using it, and want to imitate that action. So they take it.

They also swarm the farmer's fields and steal crops, as evidenced by the numerous trails leading off the fields into the woods. These are not deer trails. I have not seen one deer on any of the trails used by these creatures.

I'm not sure if they "mark" their territory, but they are the only ones I have seen using them. Each group has commuter lanes established going to their food source and water source. It is obvious they have travelled these trails countless times and beaten down the brush and broken the overhead branches for more than a generation. How many deer have been blamed and killed for farm crop loss when it was these guys instead?

BIGFOOT ON THE MOVE

I have more recently experienced the movement of a Bigfoot purely by smell. Those of you who know the experience can relate to this. The area where I noticed the smell is a reforested area, which has pine trees about 12 to 18 feet tall.

The old growth had been stripped out by lumber people and replaced with baby pine trees. They have been steadily growing for quite some time. With the exception of the occasional hunter or explorer, the area is quiet and undisturbed. This new growth area is adjacent an interstate that I travel back and forth to work on.

During the summer I was riding my motorcycle to work and noticed a stench like rotten meat near an intersection. I notice smells quicker on a motorcycle than in my truck. I guess being out in the open hits me right away, where if I am in my truck I might not notice any smell until further down the road.

It was a nice day, no breeze. I thought maybe it was a rotting carcass of a road kill, like a deer. I thought about all the deer I had seen crumpled alongside of the roads, and how the buzzards used to swarm for a free meal. I made a mental note to look tomorrow for buzzards. I thought nothing about it until the next day.

The next day I noticed the smell again, however I noted the stench had moved away from the intersection. I attributed it to maybe the wind moving in another direction, because there was a gentle breeze that day.

There were no buzzards or birds flying around the area. On the third day, I noted that the smell had moved almost a mile from the original intersection. No breeze and no reason for the smell to be that far from the intersection. This is all wooded area. And carcasses don't move unless they are being carried. When I got home I reviewed the maps again. I verified I had not tagged any prior Bigfoot activity in this stretch of woods. On the fourth day, I smelled nothing.

THE KILLJOY OF SCIENCE

I searched the fish and game rules to see where Bigfoot expeditions fall. In my state, I found out that I need a certificate to pick up a rock or log looking for a new species. Thank goodness they didn't include bricks. There's a form to fill out and I need to submit a resume of who I am and what I do and I need to write a proposal to send in with the application. And pay a fee. If I want to legally take a scat or hair sample or a stray bone from the woods, I need to apply for a scavenger certificate. That one requires a form. That one needs a written proposal too. And pay a fee.

If Bigfoot falls under the purview of a nuisance wild animal, I may be able to neutralize the danger by killing it, Of course, Bigfoot being labelled as a nuisance may be contested by law enforcement. There is a nuisance clause in the Division of Wildlife handbook that says that you can legally kill a wild animal on private property with the owner's permission if the animal is a nuisance. And if I kill one in self-defense, I would have to prove that I was in danger. That should be easy. Bears get accused all the time. You never hear someone counter that it might have been a man in a bear suit. I guess I can bag a Bigfoot on private property if I can get someone to complain.

If the Division of Wildlife finds out I bagged one, I know they will confiscate it. Two reasons. The first one is the most obvious. The folklore of Bigfoot is acceptable as a tourist draw, but the reality of a giant creature who kidnaps people and terrorizes the neighbors is not. It is better for business and less intrusive if Bigfoot remains a myth.

The second reason is that the state owns every wild animal within their boundary lines by law. Some guy just beat the state record for largest bear by hitting one with his automobile. The guy said he wanted to get it stuffed by a taxidermist, but the state game guys said no. The state confiscated it instead. Why? It is property of the state. I feel bad for this guy. I would think he would have a great story to tell everyone to explain his recently wrinkled vehicle and offset to his higher insurance premium.

What is the state going to do with it? Does the state donate the bear meat to feed the hungry? Nah, I doubt it.

What about all the fish and deer confiscated by various government officials? Every day they take the proceeds of hunters and fishermen who illegally obtained fish and game. Where does the dead animals go? The news never reports it. There is no line item in the state budget for monies received for game animals. Is it a local disposal? Is it in lock up for "safe-keeping" as evidence? Who benefits from the spoils? Maybe a shady state employee who knows a guy who can make a buck off of it? That seems more likely.

Maybe somebody in the state government has a girlfriend who is getting a nice huge bearskin rug as a present. Tough luck, dude.

BIGFOOT BAGGING

I thought about bagging one of these creatures just to prove a point that they exist. I thought about the moral dilemma, and decided that I don't think anyone I know is an animal rights advocate. It's an animal, right? I could do this. I could get out my cellphone and put the dead critter on YouTube after I whacked him. That should get the ball rolling in the right direction. It could be the newest, latest, best evidence ever. Just like the rest of the videos, only better.

I could poke him with a stick, to show he is inanimate and unmoving. I could curl his lip like Elvis, to show his monstrous yellow teeth to the camera. I could pick up and raise his big hand to the camera, like he is waving to his fans. Maybe lift a foot, to show that all the plaster casting was not done in vain. Yeah, that kind of stuff. The video would be awesome. But then I figured that I would probably get death threats from Bigfoot lovers who feel that killing Bigfoot is akin to killing a person. At least I know which ones are Bigfoot and which ones aren't. I would get a lot of views, but I would make a lot of enemies.

Then I pondered how I would drag the dead weight of a massive creature from the woods. People who hunt moose have a similar situation, I am sure. I would need a hoist, a rope and a chain. I could have that stuff ready, just in case. But the task of hauling it out…that could take all day. I don't know that I would want to hang around that long. Nighttime isn't the best time to be jacking Bigfoot's brother into my truck. Every scenario has a drawback. I could drag it out of the woods behind a vehicle, but it would get scarfed up in the transport. It might lose parts on the way out.

I could just cut its head off for forensics, and maybe its hands, because they are easy to carry and identify by someone who knows animal parts. And of course Doctor Meldrum gets a foot. All the crap he's been through, he deserves at least one for his persistence.

Nah. This plan doesn't seem so easy. As a matter of fact, it would be messy and just plain gross. Cutting up a monkey in the middle of the woods. Carrying a bunch of freezer storage bags out of the woods. If someone saw someone else carrying a head and foot and hands out of the woods, what could they think? Someone from a horror movie, right? Or a psychotic killer leaving the scene of a crime. OK, so now I have to worry about being seen while going back to my truck. I still also have to worry about Bigfoot's brother seeking revenge. This idea isn't coming together so smoothly, either.

For the sake of argument, say I succeed in getting the parts through the woods and safely drive away without repercussions. What would I do...dry ice it and ship it UPS? To whom? I earlier made a list of the ten most important people I would notify if I found some bones or a dead one. Do I send them an email, taking the best offer, or just the first offer? A phone call would be more socially proper. I could leave a message. Call now for your chance to be our Grand Prize winner. Hurry, supply is limited.

Would they graciously accept my gift to their prestigious scientific community? Or would they refuse to take it fearing ridicule from their scientific community peer group. What if my Bigfoot find doesn't fit in with their belief system? What if they have known all along? Other bodies have been reported and seized. Maybe they already have some. I don't want to be known as the guy with the Bigfoot head in his beer fridge.

I think these are problems to securing a dead body specimen as definitive proof that no one has entertained. Or they never said out loud. What's weird is that I actually thought about the choices available, and none of them are sweet. It would get downright ugly. In theory I could just hoist it up on a chain, back my truck up under it, let it down onto the truck bed and drive off. Maybe I would tarp it, maybe I might not.

I would try to drive and make my way to a prestigious university to donate the creature's body to science. Hopefully I wouldn't have to stop to refuel. That would surely raise some eyebrows.

If someone happened to call the police for me driving on the interstate with an eight foot beast in the bed of my pickup, I could deal with that. I would continue to drive with the law men right behind me, lights and siren and all. I'd drive just under the speed limit OJ style with a police escort right up to the front of the university door.

I saved the phone numbers to the various local television stations in my phone in the event that this would happen. Just in case. I would call them as I crawled along the interstate with my entourage of militarized escorts in tow. I would hope that the television news guys put a chopper in the air to get some good video footage. Now that is a story I call newsworthy!

If I get stopped on the interstate or I am forced to stop with spike strips and pepper spray, it's all over.

Regretfully, the creature's body would definitely disappear. I'm pretty sure several states already have some Bigfoot bodies in storage somewhere. They would just add one to the pile. Or maybe I'm wrong, and it goes straight to the crematorium. For the good of the people. Either way, it would be end of story.

WHO IS BEING HUNTED

People go missing in the woods every year. The internet and books abound with stories of people who knew the woods, knew their skills, and knew their odds, but never returned.

There are reasonable arguments why a trip turns ugly. A slippery slope, a loose outcropping, a deep hole or just climbing over fallen trees can ruin your day. Following animals through the woods presents its own set of obstacles, like losing your bearings and running out of daylight. In today's world, losing a signal or having a dead battery on your personal device can cause panic. Use natural clues like the suns shadow or tree moss to regain your sense of direction. If you get injured, sit down and think about what you need to do to get back to civilization.

If you see a cryptid, you will freeze. You are not froze in terror, you are basically just bewildered. Your mind holds your body still while it tries to process the scene. Even trained law enforcement report that they are struck with awe at the creature's first appearance. It seems like forever, but it only seconds. Meanwhile, your opportunity of a lifetime wanders off into the scrub brush without a picture or video to prove that it happened.

If you get the chance to use your equipment and record the event, let me be the first to congratulate you. You are now a lifelong member in the Bigfoot witness protection program. Any evidence you provide to authorities will be lost, misplaced or held for safekeeping. You will be debriefed and recommended to not disseminate your findings. Any future conversation about your sighting is not socially accepted as a bona fide hunting story and will be disavowed.

If you decide to chase wild creatures through the woods, you are on your own. The animal that you chase has more experience than you. They hunt every day, and they know their territory. You wouldn't chase rhinos and lions through tall savanna grass, and you shouldn't chase big hairy animals through the woods that can leap, swing and climb trees, either. Three seconds is an eternity when you are standing still.

There is always the unknown that no one ever thinks of. That is the one thing that will trip you up; one thing that you did not anticipate. I don't want to play the odds and lose. I am not afraid to go in the woods, but I also want to not be surprised or unprepared.

The question in my mind is this. When do you overstep your bounds by following an unknown creature with unknown behavior through the woods? Stories favor both confrontational and non-confrontational animals. Who decided to piss off whom?

When does videotaping in the interest of science turn into a frightening nightmare? They can out climb me, out maneuver me and out run me. What do you do when you become the target of their aggression? You become the next missing person story.

WORK NOTES

I would like to say I love my job, but I would be lying to you. I just set my alarm each day to go to work and get some money so that I can play. Sometimes things happen at work that can make your day. Only little things, mind you, but satisfying none the less to you. Yesterday I went outside while at work, and there was a pretty good breeze blowing in from the southwest. Normally, the wind comes in from the northeast, so this was kind of unusual.

What was more unusual was the smell. Yup! The smell of the squatch is in the air. On the other side of the building next door is a wooded area several miles long. It is the end of the industrial park. They have had activity around their drainage pond. It is outside their perimeter fence and not easily accessible from the road, but I'm not sure if it is posted. They have posted signs along the road, but maybe beyond the pond isn't their property.

I want to go there, but I'll have to walk out from work through the woods to get there, because it is a very secure facility with gates and guards. They used to manufacture microchips there, but I'm not sure what they make their now. It was vacant for a while, and I could have checked out the pond, but I didn't know back then what I know now. Now if I want to get close I have to travel about a mile through the woods around their property, and from the vegetation I see I think it is kind of swampy through there. I don't want to do any battle with Bigfoot if I'm wearing hip boots. Just saying.

I never noticed any Bigfoot activity or footprints near my work, but when I smelled the same dumpster smell as my outdoor encounter, I smiled. Ah, the smell of fresh squatch in the morning!

Note to self: Don't park near the high tension lines if the wind is blowing in this direction. They will smell me over a mile away since I can smell them from here at work. I don't know how they can smell anything over their own odor, but soap smells and fragrances are a human trait.

OK...that was a week since I wrote this. I just stepped out of the building and heard a screech. It sounded like a car sliding slowly sideswiping a telephone pole (don't ask), only much louder.

The wind is gusty from the northeast, and I smell a squatch across the main road. Not a steady stench, but wafting strong every couple of minutes. It's 4am and the road is empty.

Last week the wind was gusting from the east, and I thought the smell was traveling from where I know they live. Now it's across the road from work. My guess is that one is on the move. Welcome to the neighborhood, buddy. I'll keep my eyes peeled.

This is an update to my last paragraph. Driving in to work in the misting rain, as I turned the corner to go into the parking lot I smelled them again. There was no wind, so I knew that they were close. About an hour later I stepped outside to catch a smoke, and heard a short howl. It didn't echo due to the weather conditions, but I knew it was at least 300 yards or more to the northeast of my work building.

Some dogs to the north started barking, and I didn't hear anything more. There are houses to the north about a half mile away. I don't know if deer hunting season moved them closer to the houses for safety or not. That would be the only reason for them to move toward my work building.

SPECIES NOTES

I have started to catalog all the faces of the individual beasts I have seen. I am building quite a rogue collection of unidentified animals. I start my search by taking a picture of the terrain from a height of 150 feet to 300 feet, based on the foliage and clarity of the scene. Sometimes due to the terrain angle or the picture quality (which varies across the globe) I have to go to a higher elevation to get a nice plate of the area as a bitmap picture.

I pull this plate into a cropping capable program and crop and zoom until just the creature face is framed. Then I save this result as a .jpg file. The files are small, 1, 2 or 3 kilobytes, like a thumbnail file. I try to crop the face tightly so that you can see the facial expressions. If the face is blocked by babies (which happens a lot) or other creatures, I skip the face shot and save the body shot instead.

While I was doing this, I was listening to a rebroadcast of a Coast to Coast AM program on my computer. They cover many different topics of the unusual and unknown. On this program they were talking about a dog face beast. And I say to myself...yeah, I seen something like that... and I got a pic of one too.

So I look through the files I have cropped so far, and compare the monkey type (simian features) which is noticeably different than the ones with the protruding nose (canine features). The ones with the protruding nose could be mistaken for a werewolf in the woods, or as the radio caller suggests, a dog type face. The dog type has a narrow jawline. The monkey type has a protrusion that includes the cheeks, due to the wide set mouth and rounded jaw. The simian have noticeably large nostrils and their nose is the same color as their cheeks. It appears that a small amount of fur covers the tip.

The dog type is more canine in appearance with a narrow jaw and a short snout which comes to a point with small nostrils. Regardless of hair color, the short snout dog type nose seems to have either a tan or black tip of skin on the end. There is also a dog type seen which is long haired with a long nose and large nostrils. It is ugly compared to the short haired short snout pointy nosed ones. Their eyes are more oval than the short haired ones. Their long hair is wild looking in appearance. They will surely frighten people as they are 6 to 8 feet tall. This long haired type seems larger than the short haired variety. It has jowls that hang over its mouth on either side which gives an accentuated profile of the nose. It reminds me of a sub roll in shape. I am not sure if the short snout is a juvenile who looks ends up looking like the long hair as it gets older. Sort of like how the gray ones might be the old ones. I wish we had more scientific information.

I SEE MANY

For the purposes of this research I can see there are distinctly different kinds of unidentified creatures. There are several creatures that I am accumulating in my research that appear to be troglodyte types similar to a Neanderthal or Cro-Magnon. Some of the things I have read claim that these people must be Neanderthal. They do not appear to have the pronounced jaw and sloped large forehead like the Neanderthal. They seem more like us. They wear the skins of dead animals and wear pelts on their heads. They keep the head attached to the skin, giving the appearance of a large animal. They may easily be mistaken for a Bigfoot.

While searching in Montana and Alaska I noticed a lot of them. I'm sure they are kept warmer by the skins being used for protection from the cold. I thought they were a large furry creature until I noticed the eye holes in the pelt on their head. Then I could see their jaw exposed under the animal skin. I don't have enough information available yet to make a reasonable judgment call. They seem to be loners, and I don't want to exclude the possibility that they may be homeless squatters roaming the woods or humans who are just roaming in the woods wearing animal skins to keep warm. The yucky part is the faces of the dead animals on their pelts.

If the situation changes and they appear to be a species or a variant of animal, I will proceed accordingly. I still need to analyze more cases. I also need to examine more interaction between the simian and canine types to determine who the friend is and who the foe is. These human featured beings mingle freely with the other types.

I see that there are several unidentified species or variants of a common species here that needs official recognition and categorization. For some reason politics is keeping the research funding pool dry. Who do I ask to clear up this mystery? Bigfoot is the tip of the iceberg. I am overwhelmed with the multitude of animals I have found that I cannot identify. They are mostly big oversized furry animals.

This is such a time consuming task finding all these critters. The picture database I have compiled so far, and the field pictures represented in part in this book, represent my research. I think a variant species may be responsible for the three toed footprints being reported further south. They are big and furry and could be seen as a Bigfoot. They are in GA, LA, MS, and FL. They are as far north as NC and SC. Maybe some of the southern pictures I have are the three-toed variety. They never really show their toes to the camera. It could be a southern cousin of the Bigfoot. Or the tracks could be something completely different.

THE GLOBAL POSITIONING SYSTEM

I have begun building a database of actual photographic sightings using Google Earth as my primary resource. It is fast to resolve, easy to operate and sufficient raw data. While I used many source materials to locate and isolate viewable pictures, I found it to be convenient with their method of tagging the sighting locations. Once I had located over a thousand unusual creatures in my local area, I gave up tagging single animals. I started tagging full plates for analysis, which are large pictures of a geographic area. I just did this to keep the many map pins on my map overlay from scrunching up on my computer screen.

I have taken print screen snapshots of creatures from various county GIS, but I was never satisfied with the resolution. They did, however, get me excited by showing me the sepia ape-like images silhouetted on the GIS screen. I am surprised no one has reported seeing any creatures on their homestead maps while viewing their property on the GIS system.

For my purposes I needed a homogenous database that could cross state boundaries seamlessly, and Google Earth seemed to work for me. Did I mention that it was free? Even Google Earth Pro, a professional version, has been released for free.

I can't afford night vision goggles, and I can't afford expensive software either. So I do my research within my monetary restrictions, and do the best with what I have. As you will see if you use Google Earth, it has its limitations, but the upside is it is a digital format. By the time I frame, crop, resize and deblur, it is not the same picture, but it is still the same creature that I saw. Only better.

I'm sure that the military has better imagery on their satellite maps, but regular citizens will never get a chance to see the terrain with that kind of clarity. Some of you may remember how long it took to get a useful nonmilitary GPS product with decent accuracy. Nowadays we can't live without our GPS. We'd be lost without it. Literally.

THE UNDISCLOSED TRUTH

Maps are power in the right hands. Those who control the maps control that power. "In the interest of national security" is merely an excuse given to limit our access to decent resolution map products. I never bought into the conspiracy theorists thought process, but I've seen how government works and how power corrupts even those with the best intentions. Due to the interests of select capitalists and legislators, no one is looking into this widely reported phenomenon of strange creatures in the woods. They look the other way. Somebody with power is keeping a lid on these creatures to protect their capital ventures from being infringed.

Somebody or some collective group in Washington seems to be holding back the inevitable. As you know by now this information has been right there under our noses and visible to all, but just hasn't been acknowledged. Cause no one is actively looking. If someone ever looked they would have found Bigfoot, just like I did. Television is a public distraction provided as entertainment for us humans, and it is working as planned. It distracts you and keeps you from exploring the reality around you. Pay attention.

This story I'm telling you isn't about some public dam being delayed because of an endangered species. This story is about raising awareness of the fact that our forests and woods are filled with more than one unknown species. And yet no one is bothering to look? It has the makings of a conspiracy plot. And I am not a fan of conspiracy theorists, just someone who knows when something isn't kosher. There is more to the story than I can put here in one book. There are more levels than you or I can imagine. But I digress.

FINDING YOUR FIRST

I tried using Bing maps to compare image quality, but I wasn't happy with the clarity and definition of the resolution of the final images. I don't know the true resolution quality of Bing, and I till was able to see the creatures appear on both the map products. As I stated before, I have screen captures of creatures who were lurking on private property by viewing a county GIS map. I'm sure that you could use any map to find some creatures. Apple and MapQuest have satellite images too. It's just my personal preference to use the Google Earth product.

So to begin you start the program and watch the program open the map of the earth. Move your cursor to any North American location or select your home state, then double tap to descend downward into to the state until the state borders appear. Move your cursor to pick any location and double tap to descend downward into to the county. You should be comfortable at the 2000 foot level to begin your overview of the area. Now look hard at the map. What do you see? Roads…farms…trees. Take a minute to find a square of woods or swamp or fields that is a reasonable distance from paved roads, preferably a wooded or swampy one. Locate your cursor in the center of the square made by the roads and double tap to descend down even further into the area below. You are now far from civilization. Or at least you are a long walk to the nearest gas station. This is a good place to start. Now your search begins.

See if you can spot places to obtain food and water. Fields, wetlands and meadows are a good starting point for a food source. Streams, bogs and ponds are good examples of water sources. Even manmade ponds are a good water source. Note any proximity to an adjacent farm is considered a plus.

Next identify an old growth area of forest with large trees that have dark spaces between them. Here finding a squiggly line of a worn game trail through the forest is a plus. Lastly, double tap down once or twice more to descend into the focus range of the woods critters. You should try to get down to less than 500 feet (height of view is displayed in the left corner). Now you are ready to critter search. Look at all the pretty colors. Note the foliage texture. As you scroll your eyes will become accustomed to the foliage texture. Soon you will notice something that is not the same.

Your focus is to notice the texture that DOES NOT BELONG in the woods. Smooth areas in the jagged foliage of trees, discolored spots that obviously do not match the surrounding color of the foliage, and unusual faces or figures in the treetops or in the openings between the trees.

Bonus location is finding a game trail and scrolling along until you spot some walking down the trail. Another bonus location is at the edge of the tree line along the right-of-way of high tension electrical power lines. Scroll gently across the terrain using one direction. Scan across the screen for a light brown or tan colored spot first within the green foliage. It is similar to looking for Easter eggs in the grass. When you spot something out of the ordinary, stop scrolling and tap down to see it. If it is a primate it should look like a tan Energizer bunny with sunglasses. Congratulations! You've found your first Bigfoot!

SEARCHING IN THE SHADOWS

Use your zoom bar on the middle left to get a better view of the creature. If you can't find one after 10 minutes, go to the upper right hand corner of the map and change your compass setting to point south. It's the upper white circle. When the digital images were taken, the sun was putting a show on the terrain based on the time of day. Aligning your view to match the shadow with the trees gives you a view just like you are in the woods at the time the image was taken.

This change in the compass setting will also give you a different perspective to spot things that were invisible when your compass was set to point north. It is very useful to change your compass heading while you are checking the terrain in the ravines and valleys. Your view will change when you adjust your compass heading to a different setting. You can then check the west side straight on and then flip your compass setting 180 degrees to check the east side straight on, viewing the entire valley sides from the middle of the valley. The best view is obtained by changing the compass to align the tree shadows vertically. This will help to spot fat animals hiding behind skinny trees.

The woods are full of animals. If you can't find one in about 10 more minutes, try zooming out to ascend to the 500 feet level (display on lower right corner) and look for any odd colored spots in the trees. There may be black spots in the treetops. Those are usually babies or cubs. Because they are small, they could also be a bear cub. But if the bear cub is hang off the tree with one arm then it is probably not a bear cub. It is something else. And if you are like me and find something that gives you a first impression of monkey or ape, you have hit the jackpot.

Also you may start to recognize other animals in the woods. The woods are full of deer. If you spot a light brown animal that looks like a giraffe…that's OK…it's a deer.

The antlers on deer appear to have balls on the ends of their spikes. This may make it look funny, but it is what it is. This peculiarity seems to be caused from the limitation of resolution of the digital image (thanks to Homeland Security restrictions I guess). I'm surprised that deer hunters don't use Google Earth as a kind of fish finder for deer before they go to a new spot. Most digital map files I use are only a year or two old, and there are herds all over the woods.

SAVING YOUR IMAGES

The next step after you find an interesting scene that you want to keep is to save the image. I use the [control+print screen] function to copy the screen. This will save a copy on your computer to migrate the image into another program. Now you can paste it into Paint. Paint is a tagalong free program usually provided on most Microsoft Windows products. Open Paint and then click on File, then click on Paste, then click Save As and a screen will pop open to show you what folder you choose as your final destination for your picture. Save it as a .png or .jpg file on your computer with a name that you will remember. Now the image is saved to your files to view and crop as you choose.

I use a program called MGI Photosuite to crop my sightings. I don't think it is available for sale anymore. The website link in the program took me to a parent site, but it was not listed as for sale or download availability. What you need is a program that can crop. I would suggest using any program will do that can crop your saved pictures to give you a nice finished creature image to save.

I never sunk any money into buying the Photoshop software, so I don't know if it would have done a better job or not. If you have the money, it may help make your own Bigfoot pictures clear. A lot of people use it for photo cleanup. I only used what I had, and I had purchased my Photosuite software disc probably six or eight years ago. It does the job. Clearing up my inventory of Bigfoot pictures would be a full-time job.

I use a program called Smart Deblur to try to clear up the out of focus images that I save. I just bought the program because I was tired of looking at blurry images. How can I see their faces when they are blurry? Aren't there enough blurry pictures of Bigfoot already on the internet? This has helped me to see details in the photos that were not visible from the Google image.

So I now can deblur the image by sliding the controls until I can get a decent image. If I can't get it clear, I can always go back to my bitmap file for another zoom to another height level and then crop the new pic. Or I still have the option to go back to the map using the state designation I assigned and then find the pin number at the state level (state borders are shown as you zoom downward) to locate the scene once again. When I am happy with the result, I save the picture in my saved folder. Is there a world record for having the most blurry Bigfoot pictures? I think I could win that honor right about now. I've got a lot of un-blurring to do.

In case you were wondering, none of the hundreds of images I saved are in this book. Due to copyright restrictions, I could not use images that I cleared up and color corrected for this project. So I took my map, and drove out to see the creatures in person. And yes, they were still where the map showed them to be. Some are distance pictures, some are from video clips, and all were made using a zoom feature.

While I was cropping and resizing my road pics, I was listening to Sasquatch radio talking about Washington Bigfoot sightings. I used Google Earth to see the area he was talking about. Sure enough, Bigfoot was in the river there, splashing around with his friends. Maybe I'll send the talk show host some photos.

SEARCHING THE STREETS

I returned to New Jersey for a visit and stayed at my in-laws. I was cropping and sizing pictures on my computer when my mother-in-law asked me if there was something I wanted to watch on TV. I said no. She said she would watch anything except shows about Bigfoot. She said they are always searching and always come up with nothing. I didn't tell her I had over 1000 personal sightings sitting in my laptop.

I looked out her front window at the woods across the street and the wetlands beyond. The trees were cleared of leaves, and the underbrush was sparse as it is wintertime. About 60 acres of these woods from street to the next street are fenced off and owned by the water company. It has never been developed. I wondered if there were any creatures in there. So I checked on Google Earth. And there was. Since the area is bounded by four streets, I wondered if the street view would give me any clear view of the area. So I hit the street level tab. Sure enough, there were some creatures showing along the fence on two streets in street view. Google automatic software had blurred some, but it had missed some. Along the fence next to the high school parking lot were several standing primate types.

When I had the opportunity, I followed the streets around the fence line to see what I could see. I parked my truck in the high school parking area and got out to walk the fence line. I noticed something moving across the marsh in the tall dry grasses about half a mile away. I took out my cell phone and used the maximum zoom. I didn't see any animals. I took a photo. I walked along the fence and stopped every ten steps. I looked in a lot of trees along the fence line where Google had blurred the images, and saw nothing interesting. I took some pictures of the fence where I had seen the blurry animals. The images on Google were taken in the summer with full foliage. It was now winter and there was no foliage left on the trees and vines. I left wondering where they all went. The area looked bleak and pretty lifeless.

When I returned to my mother-in-laws house, I downloaded the phone pictures onto my computer. That is when I saw some creatures hanging out in the trees that I was just looking up at several minutes earlier. They were twenty five or thirty foot high in the trees. I looked at a lot of branches for nesting material or something out of the ordinary. But here they are. There were three more in the tall grass visible in another photo. I honestly didn't see them when I was out there on location.

I still can't believe they were visible less than ten feet from the road on Google Earth street view, and no one saw them there. Everybody looks in the city. Nobody looks at the woods?

THE FIFTY STATES PROJECT

I have accumulated several hundred pictures from VA, FL, NJ, WV, CA & OR. I have saved 15 to 20 plates showing Bigfoot type creatures representing each state. Now I have NS, SC, GA and MD added to my gallery. I am trying to get representative thumbnail pictures from every state. I have heard that there are no sightings reported in Hawaii, but I'm going to look anyway. I got 10 plates each of AZ, NM, TX, LA, MS, MO, TN and AR all in one day. Each plate had more than one Bigfoot per scene. That was over 100 Bigfoot sighted on my day off!

I opened the map in Texas while I was listening to a Bigfoot talk radio show while the caller was describing Bigfoot activity in his area. I went to the area and realized I had checked the 3D imagery block in the viewing options panel. What an awesome sight! I saved twenty plates of great Bigfoot images from a one mile wide parcel. Then I shifted closer to the airport and picked up another ten plates of great samples of the various species living in the same area.

Here is the latest 50 states update: Today I filed 15 plates in Hawaii with 10 more on Maui and 10 more in Oahu. Although there are supposedly no sightings reported in Hawaii, Bigfoot creatures do exist on the islands. Supposedly there are no sightings reported in my area of Virginia either. I know that that information is wrong. I have seen over a hundred primates in my local area appearing on the map. Most are in woods along a waterway. Some are near to the interstate in wetlands. Virginia definitely has its share of primates. So does Hawaii.

I was surprised to see that there were wildlife preserves in Hawaii. I thought everything on the islands was developed. I found creatures halfway up on the crater rim. It doesn't look like a tourist spot. It looks like a wilderness area. Now you have the knowledge to find them yourself from the comfort of your own cushy couch. How many pictures of living breathing creatures do you think we need to prove to others that something is out there? Pick a number...

This is my research so far. I know it might not be the facts as you've known them, but I am reporting to you the best information from what I see. Sure, you can judge me. I'm sure there are better pictures of the Swamp Ape or the Moth Man. I will be looking for them as well. Right now you can use this same method to search and locate Bigfoot for yourself.

I hope this book has helped solve some questions for those who want to know more, but can't find the information. I'm looking forward to others helping to expand the knowledge of Bigfoot activities and behavior. There are thousands of acres of woods and fields that need to be checked to see what Bigfoot is doing. Check in your neighborhood. Check near a farm field for Bigfoot waiting for crops to ripen. Lake heads seem to be a prime place to look for Bigfoot hunting for food.

Lately I've been listening to a Sasquatch Blog Radio show and a Bigfoot Blog Radio show while I surf the internet. I know it is just background to my primary research, which is locating species types, but I am now realizing how scared people are when they see one. There are people out there who seriously need to seek professional therapy after their experience with a Bigfoot type creature.

I hear from them that here are government guys riding around trying to play down the sightings and confiscate evidence. There is also supposedly a cleanup team to cover up when Bigfoot goes wild on campers. They are supposedly from the Forestry Service or the Department of the Interior.

I went to the Department of the Interior official website and searched "Bigfoot", but found no articles except that a Bigfoot research group was issued a citation for not obeying some park rules. All the acreage in the National Park System must not have a problem, since there are no issues to report. I think if someone from the government wanted to keep the canaries from singing, they would go about it using a better method than by imitating the Men in Black.

Maybe the forestry guys are freelancing and just riding around just trying to keep them tourist dollars flowing in to save their jobs. Or maybe the Department of the Interior is covertly involved. I guess if that was the case then their assignment would be trying to protecting their cushy government jobs as forest concierges. If they had to actually go out into the woods to do something about a Bigfoot problem, they would probably quit. I'm not a conspiracy advocate, but it sounds kind of like there might be some Bigfoot Mafia type guys driving around trying to keep everything hush-hush. Move along now. You didn't see knot-tin'! Just Fu-get-about-it!

Later, I was checking out some recently posted YouTube video and I saw that a famous group of Bigfoot hunters from television were traveling overseas to search for Bigfoot on another continent. Just for fun, I minimized the browser and opened up Google Earth again. When the globe of the earth appeared, I gave it a random spin. It spun around and around and stopped at New Zealand. I clicked and descended down to a visible level, and picked a wooded ravine. I descended further (about 800 feet) and found one! I opened a new International folder. I made a copy of the map plate and saved it in the file.

I then slid my map over the ocean area and came to the Philippine islands. I found some there on a side of a hill. Less than two minutes. Copied and saved. Next I checked in Australia, and found some on the west interior there. I think it was an aboriginal forest. Then I went to China, and found some in the lush mountains there. Copied and saved. I then went to India. Found some on a rock strewn hillside, so I copied and saved.

I knew there was Yeti, and Yowie, and Sasquatch around, but these creatures are all over! England, found some in the woodlands. Spain, found some. Morocco, found some. Every country has a little tree designator on the map that points to their National Forest. That seems to be the best place to look.

I'm going to need a bigger hard drive. My map is filling with pins. I found my thousand creatures easily. Match me if you can. This is bigger than I ever imagined. Finding Bigfoot indoors. What could be easier? Grab your favorite drink and snack, and check the local woods in your town. You might be surprised.

I'm really torn about how to get official recognition of this species. I know that some have been killed. I know that information has been collected. I know it is no secret to various government officials that something must be done. There are just too many people who have had contact. Is the answer just to bury their heads in the sand and hope that the problem will go away? Is the solution to baseline the National Parks as a refuge and relocate any strays from commercial and private land onto government protected land? Does the risk of giving them recognition change the way we do business?

I know that we are putting the two billion dollar revenue of the National Park system at risk. Who remembers what happened to the seaside businesses when the movie "Jaws" came out? Lots of people were afraid to swim in the ocean. Does the RV crowd fear Bigfoot? Hell no. Most of them probably could add some stories of their own about that hairy beast. Some city folks may decide after hearing about Bigfoot that the great outdoors isn't so great anymore. Well, no Kumbaya for them.

The campers and hikers will have to use no less caution than they do for bears or mountain lions. They would be more appropriately aware of their surroundings in the woods. Who has the largest stake in allowing a study to determine the population as it is today? And why do we spend thousands of dollars studying stupid stuff?

To recognize a creature whose habitat encompasses the entire National Park system is apparently a risk that no government official is willing to take. The safety of the citizens is second to the revenue. The incidents that occur when people and Bigfoot clash on occasion are cleansed from the official record. Bigfoot found dead by trucks and other mishaps are removed, and the official record states a deer or some other animal was involved instead. Witnesses are swayed to change their story.

Recognizing Bigfoot. It's a game. The more cards are shown, the more cards are covered. Both sides don't want to reveal their hand for fear of retribution. Both sides are fighting over ownership of the dead carcasses. But the big jackpot is truth in government. Neither side trusts the other. Both sides are trying to win. Who will be the victor? Only time will tell.